THE ART OF DreamWorks MR. PEABODY & SHERMAN

FOREWORD BY TY BURRELL

PREFACE BY TIFFANY WARD

AFTERWORD BY ROB MINKOFF

WRITTEN BY JERRY BECK

INSIGHT EDITIONS

San Rafael, California

KEN PAK

CONTENTS

Mr.Peabody & Sherman

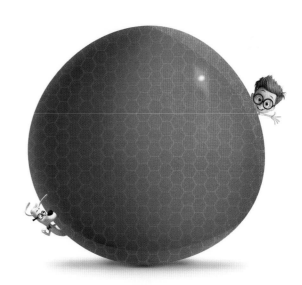

来年の夏来る

ピーボディー & シャーマン

2014年7月3日

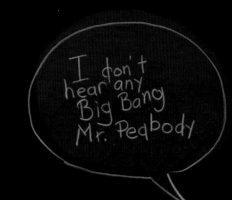

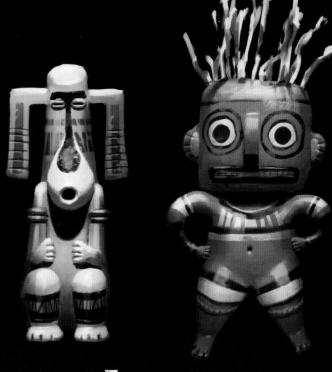

Quechua 1390-1520

Society, religion and philosophy
in pre-hispanic art

March 7 - April 12, 2014

FOREWORD
BY TY BURRELL

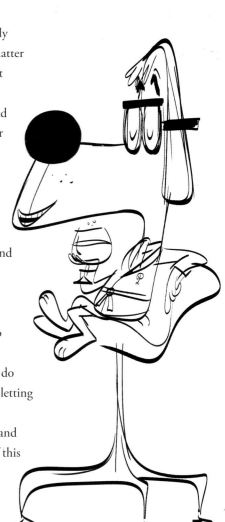

"Peabody here . . ." Actually, it's just me, the fortunate thespian honored to portray the canine genius in this incredible DreamWorks animated feature.

Traveling in time with *Mr. Peabody & Sherman* has been a nostalgic blast from my personal past. I grew up watching and laughing at all the "improbable" history from the original TV cartoons—and as a result I knew more about Benjamin Franklin, Louis Pasteur, and Ludwig van Beethoven than anyone else in my fourth-grade class. Mr. Peabody actually changed the course of my life back then, allowing me to earn straight A's in history. As Sherman might say, "Thanks, Mr. Peabody!"

Mr. Peabody was the kind of part I'd been longing to play. Here was a character I could really relate to: a self-confident super-intellectual who keeps his cool no matter how hot the circumstances. Well, maybe the opposite of me, but therein lies the acting challenge!

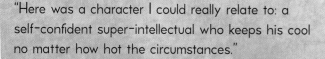

"Here was a character I could really relate to: a self-confident super-intellectual who keeps his cool no matter how hot the circumstances."

TY BURRELL

As we see in this film, being a dog is something to be proud of, and Mr. Peabody himself has quite a pedigree. The character is, of course, part of the classic Jay Ward cartoon canon, and his original voice was conceived by Ward's creative partner Bill Scott (who also did the voices for Bullwinkle and Dudley Do-Right). Mighty big shoes to fill, but thanks to the creative wizards at DreamWorks Animation, the resulting movie is nothing less than a modern-day masterpiece.

Director Rob Minkoff, who previously made animated superstars out of a certain lion cub and a particular little mouse, had a vision for the feature-length Mr. Peabody & Sherman adventure that he has now perfectly realized. As you'll see in this book, it took hundreds of artists to create the world—or should I say "worlds"—that Mr. Peabody & Sherman inhabit.

Ancient Egypt, da Vinci's Italy, revolutionary France, Peabody's elaborate penthouse—not to mention the WABAC (pronounced "way back," of course) Machine—and hundreds of historical figures from King Tut to Leonardo da Vinci; I've always wondered how the artists and animators do it, and I'm especially grateful to Rob, Alex Schwartz, Bill Damaschke, and Jeffrey Katzenberg for letting me have a front-row seat to watch it happen.

This book will allow you the same access to the preliminary paintings, production sketches, and final art that made it to the screen. It's impressive stuff, and I'm particularly proud to be a part of this funny, heart-warming, time-twisting picture.

Or as Mr. Peabody says in the film, "I think we can file this under 'unqualified success.'" Indeed!

1 • SHANE PRIGMORE

2–4 • CRAIG KELLMAN

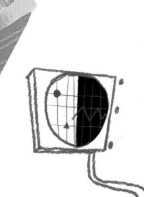

PEABODY & SHERMAN

PREFACE
BY TIFFANY WARD

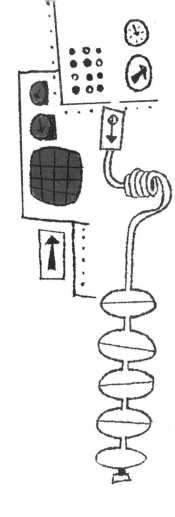

My father, Jay Ward, originally produced Mr. Peabody & Sherman in 1959 for the launch of "Rocky and His Friends" on ABC television (renamed "The Bullwinkle Show" when it moved to NBC prime time in 1961). The cartoon series aired an episode of "Rocky and Bullwinkle" at the head and tail of each half hour with various five-minute segments mixed in between. The segments included "Mr. Peabody & Sherman," "Fractured Fairy Tales," "Dudley Do-Right," and "Aesop and Son." The entire show was produced at Ward Productions, Inc., where my dad had his imprint on everything that happened.

My dad died way too young at the age of sixty-nine in 1989. As his only daughter—sandwiched between two brothers—I have had the good fortune to run Dad's company for the last twenty-four years. My dad was truly a genius as well as a very unique and eccentric person who saw humor in everything surrounding him! He believed that life was tough and that humor made it so much better. He would be *so* proud that his legacy of humor lives on in this new movie, releasing fifty-five years after its television launch.

There are many things you may not know about Jay Ward and his studio. In addition to his unique sense of humor, I think of Dad as the first great promotions specialist. He wanted more advertising than the networks provided to promote his show—so he created and financed waves of newsworthy promotions many years before it became common. Some of his more memorable stunts included:

- Blocking off Sunset Boulevard for a block party to unveil the Rocky and Bullwinkle statue. Bullwinkle wore a bathing suit and held Rocky in his hand, mimicking the Stardust Hotel Girl billboard across the street. She rotated endlessly, so Rocky and Bullwinkle did as well. The sheriff of Los Angeles attended, as well as Jayne Mansfield and other celebrities. Everyone had to dress in period costume from the 1920s.

- A picnic at the Plaza Hotel in New York, where he rented the entire ballroom and hired fake pickpockets along with ants in containers and box lunches.

- Hosting celebrity elbow-bending ceremonies under the Bullwinkle and Rocky statue to mimic Grauman's Chinese Theatre's foot and handprints.

"There could be no greater tribute to my father, Jay Ward, than bringing his characters to life again and introducing them to a new generation."

TIFFANY WARD

DANGER

PHOTO CREDIT: THE WARD FAMILY

⊙ Mounting a circus calliope on a van and traveling cross-country doing TV and radio shows and getting signatures for "Moosylvania as the 51st state." He arrived at the White House to submit the signed petitions on the day the Cuban Missile Crisis broke out. Dad said, "Boy—they weren't friendly" when he was turned away at the White House gates!

⊙ Carrying out Operation Loudmouth, a series of very, very funny one sheets sent to heads of networks, studios, and advertisers on a wide variety of subjects—just to promote Ward Productions, Inc., in the hopes of getting more series on the air and making famous the ones he had on.

But my favorite event was one he made particularly special and fun: my wedding. There were many hysterical surprises that made me laugh and warmed my heart:

⊙ A 1919 Rolls Royce and chauffeur (partitioned driver separate) took us from the church to the reception at the Riviera Country Club. As we drove from the church to the reception, skywriters decorated the blue sky with CONGRATULATIONS TIFFANY AND JIM.

⊙ A dummy dressed to look like my dad that stood in our receiving line armed with comedy lines composed by his writers but spoken by my dad. It was the longest receiving line I've ever experienced as the guests went through repeatedly to catch all the funny lines.

⊙ And the pièce de résistance: Dad built a platform on the Riviera Country Club so that the Goodyear Blimp could be our going-away vehicle!

As president of Ward Productions, president of Bullwinkle Studios, and executive producer on *Mr. Peabody & Sherman,* I have been honored to be a part of this labor of love and see Dad's highly respected property transformed into a fabulous movie. Working with the filmmakers and artists at DreamWorks Animation has been a spectacular experience and one of pure pleasure and respect. Rob Minkoff is a brilliant leader, and I feel privileged to have him as director and friend. There could be no greater tribute to my father, Jay Ward, than bringing his characters to life again and introducing them to a new generation.

DOG IN MOTION (WITH TIE AND SPECTACLES)
20TH JUNE, 1878

INTRODUCTION
"PEABODY HERE"

*"Sherman—set the WABAC Machine for 1959.
Destination: Hollywood, California."*

With those words, we begin our journey back to a time when animation producer Jay Ward was about to introduce two of his most famous characters to America: a flying squirrel named Rocky and his pal, Bullwinkle J. Moose. When they made their television debut on November 19, 1959, however, they were not alone. Along for the ride were Mr. Peabody, a time-traveling dog, and his red-headed boy, Sherman.

According to the show's title, Jay Ward and his head writer and co-producer, Bill Scott, pictured "Rocky and His Friends" as an animated variety show featuring several different episodes each week. Perhaps the most beloved of these was "Peabody's Improbable History." Mr. Peabody & Sherman didn't just travel through time; they actually participated in major events featuring some of the most famous figures in history. In fact, if not for Mr. Peabody's WABAC Machine and his superior intellect, the world as we know it today might not exist!

First, Mr. Peabody had to be brought to life. Ted Key was a successful magazine cartoonist best known for his clever comic *Hazel*. Key sketched up a story of a child who could time travel. The boy was named Danny Daydream, and he had a pet dog named Beware. ("Beware the Dog," get it?) Key submitted this to his brother Leonard, who was working for Jay Ward as a salesman. For comedy's sake, Ward and Scott reversed Key's concept so that it became a genius dog who had a pet boy. The journeys through history remained, and a time machine, the WABAC Machine, was added by Ward. The dog was renamed after Scott's own pet beagle, Peabody, and Danny became Sherman, after an animation director Scott once worked with at UPA.

Bill Scott was the voice of Mr. Peabody, basing him on the erudite 1940s movie character Mr. Belvedere, as portrayed by actor Clifton Webb. Sherman was voiced by an adult actor named Walter Tetley. Tetley had made his reputation in radio playing young, sarcastic wise guys, but for Sherman he came up with a voice suggesting a wide-eyed naïf who would follow his canine caretaker to the ends of time.

Bill Scott wrote the first episode featuring an encounter with Napoleon, but writing duties soon fell to Chris Hayward. There seemed to be only two rules to the episodes: First, no historical figure, however great, could solve any problem without the timely help of Mr. Peabody. Second, there must be puns by the tons. Each of the ninety-one episodes, in fact, ends in a most outrageous pun.

> "I was asked if I was interested in directing a movie version of Mr. Peabody & Sherman, and without hesitation I said, 'Absolutely yes!'"
>
> ROB MINKOFF, DIRECTOR

1 • CARLOS FELIPE LEÓN

2 • CRAIG KELLMAN

3 • SHANE PRIGMORE

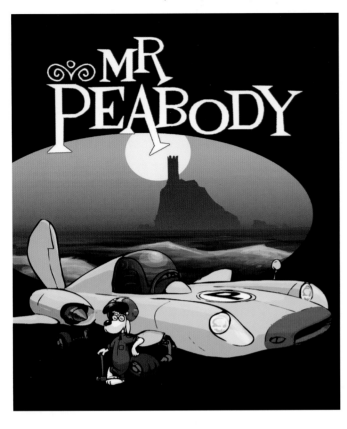

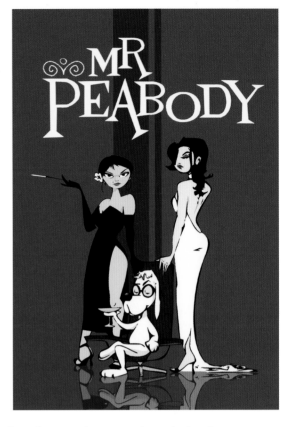

1

2

3

4

King Arthur, Jesse James, Henry VIII, Beethoven—Mr. Peabody & Sherman met them all and dozens more in some of the wittiest cartoons ever written for television. Mr. Peabody may have had a large ego, but nobody did more for civilization than this brilliant white dog in a red bow tie. If "Rocky and His Friends" is remembered today as one of television's greatest cartoon shows, part of the credit undeniably belongs to Mr. Peabody & Sherman, time travelers extraordinaire.

Cut to 2003. Jay Ward's daughter, Tiffany Ward, began to explore the idea of a Mr. Peabody movie. Working with the development executives at Classic Media, they set up a meet-and-greet with director Rob Minkoff, whose credits include *The Lion King* and *Stuart Little*. "I was asked if I was interested in directing a movie version of Mr. Peabody & Sherman, and without hesitation I said, 'Absolutely yes,'" recalls Minkoff. "I didn't really know at that time what that would be or what it would mean, but I loved the characters."

Love is a key ingredient that carried this project through to its completion. "I love Jay Ward, and I was a big fan of Mr. Peabody & Sherman," says Minkoff. "I was a fan of it for a number of reasons, not the least of which, it was such a great way as a kid to be exposed to all sorts of history I knew nothing about. For that reason alone, it seemed like it was a great idea to revive these characters."

Producer Alex Schwartz, who previously worked with DreamWorks CEO Jeffrey Katzenberg at Disney, first became attached to the project when she did some preliminary development with Minkoff for independent producer Walden Media. "Rob Minkoff and his producing partner, Jason Clark, originally brought the project to Walden, who had to drop out after a few years," Schwartz recalls. But Minkoff never lost his faith in the project's potential. The director brought the concept to Katzenberg at DreamWorks in 2005, and the studio head immediately saw its possibilities. Schwartz had moved over to DreamWorks in the interim, and Katzenberg quickly reunited the pair to make the film a reality.

However, getting the go-ahead turned out to be the tricky part. "In fact, the very first script was an entirely different story with an entirely different set of characters," says Minkoff of an early draft written by Andrew Kurtzman. "After months spent developing and hammering out that first script, it was back to the drawing board." Two new writers, Joshua Sternin and Jeff Ventimilia, came in and pitched a new twist, a fresh idea that would sideline all of the previous thinking. "We ended up doing another draft and got a green light on that," Minkoff continues, "but they had to leave on another assignment. And then Craig Wright joined us, and later, Michael McCullers. From there it was completely remade into the film it is today." Such is the nature of feature animation.

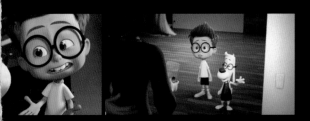

1 • KEN PAK, PRISCILLA WONG, CARLOS FELIPE LEÓN,
RUBEN PEREZ, AVNER GELLER & TIM LAMB

2 • TIM LAMB

1

Enter the DreamWorks Animation team. Production was split between the studio's Glendale campus and Redwood City facility. In the case of recruiting a creative crew within DreamWorks, it wasn't hard to find enthusiastic fans of the original Mr. Peabody & Sherman cartoons.

"I think when we first heard the Mr. Peabody & Sherman pitch we were taken with the possibilities of both the smarts and the slapstick inherent in the characters," said DreamWorks Animation chief creative officer Bill Damaschke. "The potential to have incredibly smart writing, really funny situations involving historical characters, the innocence and charm of Sherman and the wit of Mr. Peabody—it just felt like such a great show."

Many who worked on the movie cited that very first television episode that explained how Peabody adopted Sherman, and how they fell in love with the quirky premise of a talking dog adopting a boy. "When you see a 2D classic like that," as art director Tim Lamb puts it, "you can immediately see the potential for adapting the themes of Peabody's story into a much bigger adventure. Even as we considered how to treat the film stylistically, there were pieces of the classic that we wanted to retain in the film."

If Rob Minkoff and Alex Schwartz had one goal, it was to capture the spirit of the original series while bringing Mr. Peabody & Sherman up-to-date in the age of digital filmmaking—and

the kind of theatrical entertainment modern audiences expect. Minkoff remembers the challenge: "It couldn't be a slavish copy of the original. You want to take the best of what people remember about the show and expand upon it, while always trying to be true to the spirit of the characters."

> "Mr. Peabody is a genius who's prepared for everything, thought everything through, has everything figured out except how a kid is going to behave."
>
> BILL DAMASCHKE, DREAMWORKS ANIMATION CCO

Admiring the original characters, however, was not enough. Mr. Peabody & Sherman still had to star in a movie that took their unique charm into uncharted territory. Head of story Walt Dohrn explains, "The spirit of the original Ward cartoons was really important to us. We needed to pay homage to that sensibility, but also to tell a grander story that had to be a little richer for today's audience."

Although it was determined early in production that time travel would play a major role in the film's plot, the filmmakers

quickly settled on what would become the movie's central theme: the special bond between Mr. Peabody & Sherman, perhaps the most nontraditional family ever to star on-screen. Schwartz realized that this was the crucial aspect of the Mr. Peabody & Sherman saga: "The DNA of these characters is that of an unconventional family. The very fact that Jay Ward nods to it in the show and has a judge validate the adoption is part of who they are."

The DreamWorks team had to consider angles that never would have come into play in a more traditional film. "If a boy can adopt a dog, I see no reason why a dog can't adopt a boy," ruled the judge in the very first cartoon. Logical, perhaps, but leaving several questions for the film to answer: What does it mean to be Mr. Peabody, a dog who adopts a boy, even with the blessings of the court? What is it like to be a single dog who has a son?

One idea forwarded by Damaschke suggested that for once, the brilliant Mr. Peabody didn't have *all* the answers: "Mr. Peabody is a genius who's prepared for everything, thought everything through, has everything figured out except how a kid is going to behave or what a kid will actually end up doing with his life." The DreamWorks team thus developed Mr. Peabody as a caring, if somewhat confused, parent, even though he has certain personality quirks that make him, at times, highly sensitive, self-important, but unexpectedly tender. And Sherman? He believes in his canine father completely.

Another theme that lent drama to the story was the fact that not everyone would be accepting of this most nontraditional of families. Something needed to come between Peabody and his son, and so Craig Wright suggested the character of Miss Grunion to personalize the intolerance that an extraordinary family could encounter in the real world.

Damaschke nicely summed up how the production team felt about the original characters and the wonder of making a film about a most unusual time-traveling duo: "Mr. Peabody & Sherman really stand out. It's a unique concept: a dog who talks and who's also a genius. It's never really explained, but you just go with it. You're in the movie, you believe in their situation, and you're enjoying it!"

Some of the irrepressible fun will shine through in unexpected ways. Hopefully, you will notice that when Mr. Peabody & Sherman visit King Tut's Egypt, the hieroglyphs are all cartoons and funny little messages. As Lamb playfully informs us, "You will have to watch the movie several times to find a few visual gags that pay tribute to characters from other Jay Ward creations."

The DreamWorks team inherited a classic television cartoon and retained its original spirit while adding a fresh dose of adventure, fun, and heart. Now we are ready to have the WABAC Machine transport us to meet an incredible cast of characters.

7:30 AM

7:34 AM

MR. PEABODY

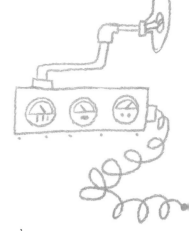

Celebrated, cultured, manicured, and clipped. Mr. Peabody, the epitome of cool, has seen and done it all. Nobel Prize–winning scientist, adviser to heads of state, world-renowned explorer, Olympic gold medalist in the long jump and decathlon—no dog has ever achieved more. And in perhaps his biggest adventure, Peabody tackles his greatest challenge: parenthood.

As if capturing the personality of Mr. Peabody weren't challenge enough, director Rob Minkoff and his team of designers were also faced with adapting a beloved two-dimensional, hand-drawn, limited

> "I always thought of Peabody as a teacher. . . . And yet there's something whimsical, something more Willy Wonka-ish about him than your average classroom instructor."
>
> ROB MINKOFF, DIRECTOR

animation cartoon into a three-dimensional character. No one had any desire to reinvent the essential traits that made Mr. Peabody great. "I said, 'I'm really not interested in doing this project if we modernize or recreate Mr. Peabody & Sherman without regard to the original material,'" says production designer David James. "So rest assured our Mr. Peabody remains very much the completely urbane, sophisticated character you always knew and loved."

Director Minkoff knew that retaining the original character's trademarks was important, but they had to make sense within the new world created for the film. "We tried to add plausibility to the design of the whole thing," he says. "A film project usually begins with the main character and what you're trying say. We have a dog that talks and walks around, that wears a bow tie and not much else. But the fact that he's a character in this world, you sort of have to create a world that he fits into, that he belongs in."

The overall design must reflect, in shorthand, who the character is. "I always thought of Peabody as a teacher," says Minkoff. "That's what he always was on the original show. And yet there's something whimsical, something more Willy Wonka–ish about him than your average classroom instructor."

Genius and historian, Mr. Peabody has traveled not only the world but throughout time, so he knows everybody and has seen everything. With a character like that, how do you challenge him? Minkoff gave

that a lot of thought: "The one thing that you cannot really be a genius about is how unpredictable kids can be. Whatever you try isn't going to work." What does work is Peabody's final design, which incorporates the basics of the original Jay Ward style into a pleasing, fully rounded personality. "One of the things that we started off with was a much more rectilinear, squared-off Mr. Peabody," recalls James. "In character designer Craig Kellman's early designs, we really liked the idea of having his glasses actually being incorporated into his expressions."

Mr. Peabody's point of view plays an important role in visualizing the inner workings of his mind. As Mr. Peabody explains his solutions, the screen shows us his strategy via various arrows, circles, info text, and other visual details. Head of story Walt Dohrn tells of how they came up with "Peabody Vision": "We were looking for a unique way to show how Peabody can get out of a situation, and it was fun to kind of do it retroactively. We did that because Peabody's plans were so complex—and so smart. We needed to see his logic in real time, so we came up with this idea to go inside the mindscape of Peabody and see the equations."

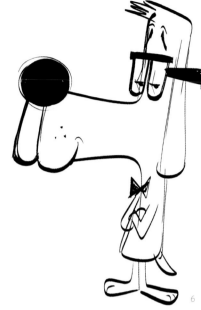

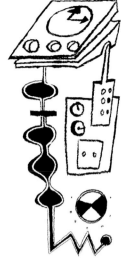

1, 2 • CRAIG KELLMAN

3 • SHANE PRIGMORE

4–6 • CRAIG KELLMAN

7 • CARLOS FELIPE LEÓN

"The one thing that you cannot really be a genius about is how unpredictable kids can be. Whatever you try isn't going to work."

ROB MINKOFF, DIRECTOR

1–4, 6 • CRAIG KELLMAN

5 • SHANE PRIGMORE

SHERMAN

When a dog like Mr. Peabody adopts a boy, it's certain that boy must be someone very special. A bit shy, but always up for adventure. Smart, but naïve about life. A boy able to handle the attention that comes with being raised in an unusual family and comfortable enough to love being part of it. We're talking, of course, about Sherman, Mr. Peabody's energetic young "son."

Ever since Mr. Peabody adopted Sherman as an infant, the boy has shared his "dad's" penchant for time travel. Before he ever set foot in school, Sherman had witnessed more history than his classmates would learn in a lifetime. If Sherman tells someone that George Washington never chopped down a cherry tree, well, it's because Sherman learned it firsthand.

> "It was interesting having Sherman deal with the real world and seeing the complications of life, something that the original show really didn't touch on."
>
> WALT DOHRN, HEAD OF STORY

Production designer David James hints at Sherman's unique personality in the way the character is animated: "Peabody is quite refined, smooth, controlled in his movement, whereas Sherman is just the opposite, more squash and stretch, sort of all over the place. He's like a pony or a puppy, not quite grown into his body. That's why he and Mr. Peabody play so well off each other, with Sherman being pure energy while Mr. Peabody is the epitome of control."

Although Sherman takes some teasing due to having Mr. Peabody as his dad, he truly loves the brilliant dog and looks to him for guidance. That can be quite a job, since parenting a child is one mystery that Mr. Peabody hasn't completely solved. Head of story Walt Dohrn says, "It was interesting having Sherman deal with the real world and seeing the complications of life, something that the original show really didn't touch on."

1 • TIM LAMB

2–5 • CRAIG KELLMAN

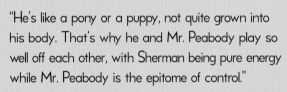

"He's like a pony or a puppy, not quite grown into his body. That's why he and Mr. Peabody play so well off each other, with Sherman being pure energy while Mr. Peabody is the epitome of control."

DAVID JAMES, PRODUCTION DESIGNER

In order to portray such a boy, director Rob Minkoff insisted from the beginning that a child actor would give Sherman a voice. According to Dohrn, "That really added so much to the charm and reality of Sherman, exactly what we wanted to get with the naïveté and playfulness that real kids have."

Presenting Sherman as a visual character took the art crew back to the designs used in the original cartoon series. "Sherman has an enormous head," observed Minkoff, "so we decided to keep that design because we wanted him to be recognizable from the character in the cartoon. If you look at the original drawings, his head is even bigger and his body is tiny and skinny, so it was a challenge to translate Sherman into three dimensions." James emphasized another visual trick that links Mr. Peabody to Sherman: "Their big, round, Philip Johnson glasses."

Whether Sherman is visiting ancient Egypt or Renaissance Italy, or marveling at the Trojan Horse, the boy who belongs to a genius dog is one of the most engaging movie creations in recent memory. Designed and animated with irresistible appeal, it's not hard to see why Mr. Peabody took Sherman under his paw.

1, 3 • CRAIG KELLMAN

2 • SHANNON TINDLE

"Sherman is a seven-year-old kid who totally believes in his father one hundred percent. He's an optimist, completely open to all experiences, excited about learning, and excited about the world."

JASON SCHLEIFER, HEAD OF CHARACTER ANIMATION

PENNY

When we meet Penny Peterson during Sherman's first day of school, she's the sharp, snarky leader of a clique of mean girls. She quickly acquires a personal grudge against the know-it-all Sherman and also begins to accuse him of being a dog—after all, he does bite her on the first day they meet.

Penny is a complex, unpredictable little lady, conforming to no one's idea of a typical sweet little girl (except maybe her parents', Paul and Patty Peterson). She serves as the catalyst for the movie's key time-traveling adventure, as well as a surrogate for the audience as they enter Mr. Peabody & Sherman's world.

Penny's character design became a crucial element bridging the preexisting designs of Mr. Peabody & Sherman to the world created for the rest of the film. Character designer Joe Moshier had to make sure the design of Penny would look and feel proper next to Sherman. "Penny gave us the foundation for all the background

characters," says Moshier. "I referenced Sherman's design, his overall aesthetic—his big rectangular-shaped head versus his real thin limbs. I wanted Penny to reflect that idea as well." During the course of the film, Penny goes from being a bratty schoolgirl to portraying an Egyptian princess. By the film's conclusion, she matures into a true friend. That range of personality had to be reflected in her final design.

> "She starts off as a mean girl, one of the top in the political hierarchy of seven-year-olds and eight-year-olds. And she's quite smart."
>
> JASON SCHLEIFER, HEAD OF CHARACTER ANIMATION

1 • TIM LAMB

2 • JOE MOSHIER

"Penny has quite a big arc through the film," says Jason Schleifer, head of character animation. "It was important for us to make her immediately appealing, even though she starts the film as a villain. Sherman, on the other hand, is a really nice and likeable person. He's open, naïve, and a bit innocent. We had to keep pushing Penny's performance to make it incredibly aggressive in order for him to snap and do something completely out of character. However, without the initial appeal, it would have been difficult to make her arc believable." Moshier adds, "I really focused on the overall silhouette of her hair and her eyes, just to make sure that she could be someone we'd care about."

Balance in Penny's character was essential, especially in considering her dynamic with Sherman. And that balancing act led to a curious discovery. "With Penny there was an interesting little thing I happened to notice, possibly by design," says production designer David James. "It's Penny who entices Sherman on this adventure, drawing him to this experience by goading him into taking the WABAC Machine. It wasn't intentional, but there is a bit of Adam and Eve in their relationship—and there is also a bit of the apple: the red orb of the WABAC. It's a coincidence, born in the truth of the moment—and it's probably why it works."

"Penny gave us the foundation for all the background characters. I referenced Sherman's design, his overall aesthetic—his big rectangular-shaped head versus his real thin limbs. I wanted Penny to reflect that idea as well."

JOE MOSHIER,
CHARACTER DESIGNER

THESE PAGES • JOE MOSHIER

45

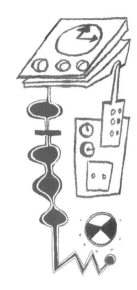

2

THE PETERSONS

Penny's parents, the Petersons, play a small but vital role in the story. Mr. Peabody needs to win them over to smooth things over between Sherman and Penny, as well as with himself and Miss Grunion. Inviting the Petersons over for dinner, some drinks, and a little music should have done the trick—and might have if Sherman hadn't introduced Penny to the WABAC Machine.

As head of character animation, Jason Schleifer had fun dissecting the Petersons' personalities: "Stephen Colbert is playing Paul, the dad, and he's interesting because he's an intensely distracted father. It was a great animation exercise trying to demonstrate a character who is one hundred percent committed to whatever he's focused on—until his focus shifts and then he commits one hundred percent to the new idea."

And then there's Mom, Patty (voiced by Leslie Mann), who's very supportive of her husband. "She realizes that he has a tough job, he gets distracted, and she's there for him," says Schleifer. "There's a scene where Peabody says something really witty and Paul just doesn't react. He goes blank and Patty covers for him, 'Isn't that funny? That's really

funny. He's not a big laugher.' That's the way that she is. When Patty reacts it's big, wide-open, really appealing, and very positive."

Unfortunately, the stress of his daily life causes Paul to have back spasms. Luckily, Mr. Peabody is a licensed chiropractor and soon has Paul in the palm of his paw. "Animator Nedy Acet animated Paul's spasmodic contortions and pushed the cartoonier side of the character animation," recalls Schleifer. "It's always great taking the movement and poses to this extreme." Penny remains the most important thing in the Petersons' lives—and the girl clearly gets her personality from both parents. "I feel Penny's behavior, at least in the beginning, is largely based off her father more than her mother," says Schleifer. "Her reactions to Mr. Peabody & Sherman, and the way she treats the world around her, definitely demonstrate more of her father's personality. By the end of the film, Penny gets a bit more supportive and skews more toward her mother's personality. It ties the three of them together."

The Petersons also represent a different, more traditional family unit than that of Mr. Peabody & Sherman. No less important—but just as funny.

1 • TIM LAMB

2 • RUBEN PEREZ

45

PRISCILLA WONG

PEABODY'S PAD

Where else would one of the world's biggest brains reside? In the original cartoon series from the 1960s, Mr. Peabody & Sherman lived in a penthouse on top of a steel-and-glass skyscraper. For the movie, that idea simply had to be expanded. "We took it a step further that maybe he lives in the ultimate mélange of modern architecture," says production designer David James. "And we added to its excess by making his home a penthouse on top of the tallest skyscraper in Central Park South."

Of course, the building he lives atop is the worldwide headquarters of that celebrated think tank, Peabody Industries. According to James, "Our first idea was that he lived in this beautiful modern house in the country." That didn't make sense for one who is the brains behind some of the world's greatest scientific discoveries. Peabody was clearly an urbanite, with access to the greatest museums and schools, the fine arts, and the latest technology. "In the end, Peabody's city home is a combination of architecture's greatest hits."

The interior is a very contemporary, retro-styled, midcentury modern living space, accessorized with souvenirs carefully collected over a lifetime of adventures. "He is a traveler, very literally a time traveler," says James of Peabody's interior décor. "He has been everywhere and every*when*, so he has this collection of impossible artifacts, amazing art, and gifts from the greatest figures in history."

RUBEN PEREZ

But even within a space so cluttered with antiquities, there has to be order. "We discussed the background of every objet d'art, as well as functional items," recalls James. "We talked about how if Mr. Peabody would have a bar set, it would be from the golden age of drinking. He would have probably had a cocktail with Dorothy Parker. . . . The shaker that he is using, he would never simply go to one of our typical home stores, you know? He would go and get the original—and that is the sort of underpinning of all the stuff in his place." Peabody's material possessions reflect the cultured canine that he is—and that's the basis of his home's interior decoration. "I am a great believer in design taking a backseat to character," says James. "Hopefully those things just add a little sprinkle of hints about who he is, without being too deliberate."

1 • CARLOS ZARAGOZA

2 • RUBEN PEREZ

3, 4 • KORY HEINZEN

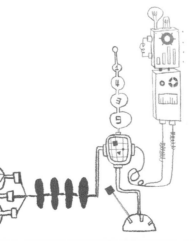

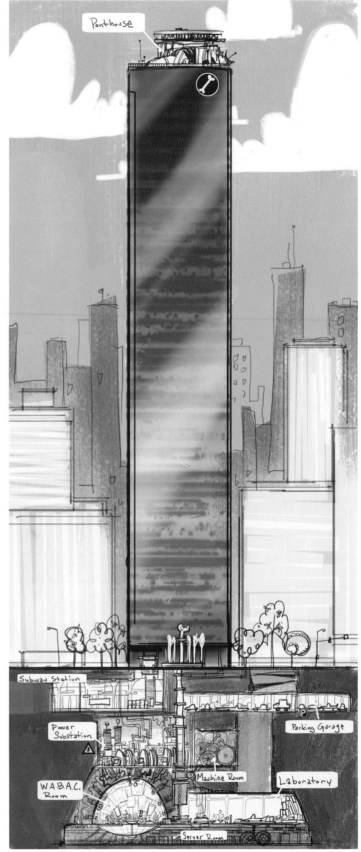

PEABODY INDUSTRIES

THESE PAGES • KORY HEINZEN

1 • DAVID JAMES & MICHAEL MAO   4 • ALEX PUVILLAND

2, 3 • ZAC WOLLONS   5 • DAVID JAMES

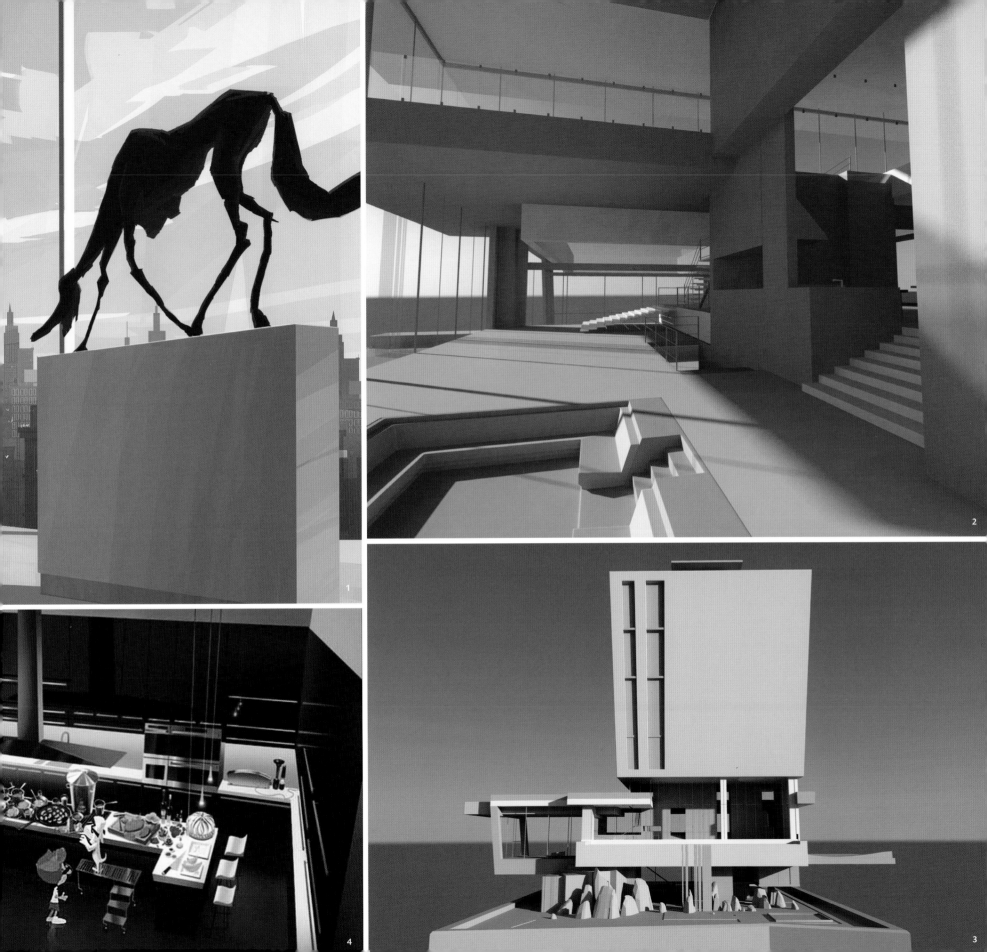

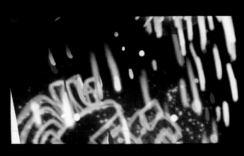

THESE PAGES • KORY HEINZEN

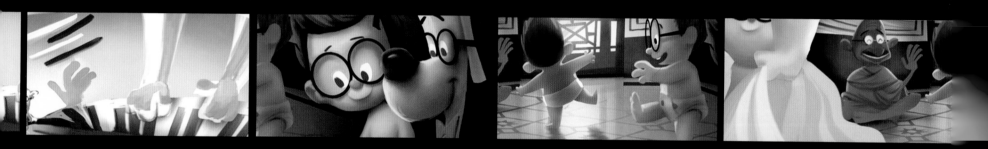

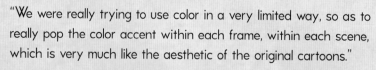

"We were really trying to use color in a very limited way, so as to really pop the color accent within each frame, within each scene, which is very much like the aesthetic of the original cartoons."

DAVID JAMES, PRODUCTION DESIGNER

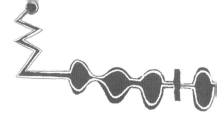

1 • PASCAL CAMPION

2 • CARLOS FELIPE LEÓN

3 • CRAIG KELLMAN

SHERMAN'S ROOM

S ometimes it's the smallest details that can tell so much about a
character. Sherman's bedroom is indeed cluttered with details
that tell us what he loves and who he wants to be. Like any
red-blooded little boy, Sherman has action figures, posters, and books
strewn about—and, of course, an unmade bed.

Unlike Mr. Peabody's well-curated collections and objets d'art,
Sherman's toy collection at first glance seems less thought-out.
However, production illustrator Alex Puvilland's visual development
paintings reveal, perhaps on a subconscious level, that Sherman's
favorite playthings are transportation devices—not unlike the WABAC
Machine—which include race cars, sailing ships, rockets, and trains.

It's here in Sherman's room that Mr. Peabody tucks him in at
night, where they have heart-to-heart talks and where, in the film,
Sherman tells Peabody of the events of his first day of school—the
very events that set the whole film in motion.

THESE PAGES • PRISCILLA WONG

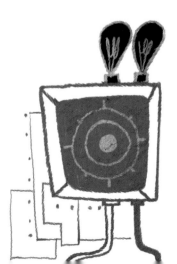

1, 2 • ALEX PUVILLAND

3 • KORY HEINZEN

2

3

SHERMAN'S SCHOOL

ven the design of an intentionally mundane location like Sherman's school plays an integral part in telling the story and provides insight into the characters' feelings.

Sherman attends an austere private school narrowly sandwiched between the brownstones in the middle of Manhattan. "The school is really designed to go from a very happy, sunny experience—as when Sherman is dropped off by his father—to that isolating experience of first integrating into a peer group," says production designer David James. "I think everyone feels a little bit like Sherman on their first day in a new place."

Color design is an important factor here, as it sets the tone for the conflict to come. "Sherman is the only splash of red in the school—which is meant to delineate and underpin how he is slightly removed from the other children when he arrives," says James. But by the time he arrives in the lunchroom scene, where Penny and Sherman have a confrontation, a lot of color—that is to say, the warmth—has been removed from the environment.

Ultimately Sherman's school is like every school everywhere. It inspires kids to want to go home and hang out with their dog.

1 • KORY HEINZEN

2 • PRISCILLA WONG

MISS GRUNION

"He bit her," says Miss Grunion, the relentless social worker from the Bureau of Child Safety and Protection. A towering, stern Valkyrie, Miss Grunion is all business when it comes to Sherman. No matter what famous feats Mr. Peabody has accomplished, she is already convinced that no dog, however brilliant, should adopt a boy. When Sherman bites his classmate Penny during a scuffle, Miss Grunion sees an opening to remove Sherman from Mr. Peabody's custody—permanently.

"Miss Grunion is quite literally monolithic," says production designer David James. "Her shape and characterization is of an intractable, slablike, powerful thing. She was designed to be a hulking presence, a guardian for the preservation of what she considers to be 'the rules.'"

"Miss Grunion came to the situation representing those who aren't very tolerant of something that's unique or out of the ordinary," says head of story Walt Dohrn. "I like that idea for a villain since Peabody is someone thinking beyond—or even working outside—the typical conventions of society. We introduce her in the first act so that you know what the stakes are and you don't forget her. When she comes back and threatens to arrest Peabody and take Sherman away, it's a real thing. Miss Grunion is totally bad, and she's a real threat. She's pretty scary."

1 • CARLOS FELIPE LEÓN

2 • BRYAN LASHELLE

3 • KORY HEINZEN

4–6 • TIM LAMB

7 • CHIN KO

1 • PRISCILLA WONG

2 • STEVIE LEWIS

3, 4 • TIM LAMB

TEACHERS, STUDENTS, AND OTHER CONSIDERED CHARACTERS

Like any epic story spanning several centuries, the film's artists and designers had to come up with a literal cast of thousands. Not all of these characters have big parts or even speaking roles. But all of them enhance the story, amplify the visuals, and simply add to the fun.

Art director Tim Lamb—who designed, among many other characters, Miss Grunion—realized this production would be a character designer's paradise: "Right away I was drawn toward this film because of the vast amount of characters and the different historical locations we visit."

Sherman's friend Carl, like the crowds of kids at his school, had to have a unified caricatured design in order to fit with Mr. Peabody's & Sherman's established looks. Visual development artist Priscilla Wong created templates for generic men; Lamb and character designer Joe Moshier came up with a model for generic women. Key features from these—such as nose forms, head shapes, and body structures—were individually finessed to create dozens of "extras" for the crowd scenes.

One standout character was the principal of Sherman's private school, Purdy. "He is a nervous, sweaty, globe-headed little bureaucrat with a bad comb-over, in charge of running Sherman's school the best he can," says production designer David James. "He has some sympathy for the situation Peabody is in, but there was no possible way for him to go against Grunion—the character he was originally designed to play against."

In addition to all the historical figures in the time-travel sequences, the film includes policemen, TV reporters, taxicab drivers, and crowds of spectators. "I love characters and I love character design," says Lamb, "and this movie was just the perfect vehicle for exploring a wide range of characters. Whether in ancient times or contemporary settings, there would be a wide variety of character types. Everything from modern day New Yorkers to Egyptian rulers, French Revolutionaries . . . not to mention a bespectacled talking dog."

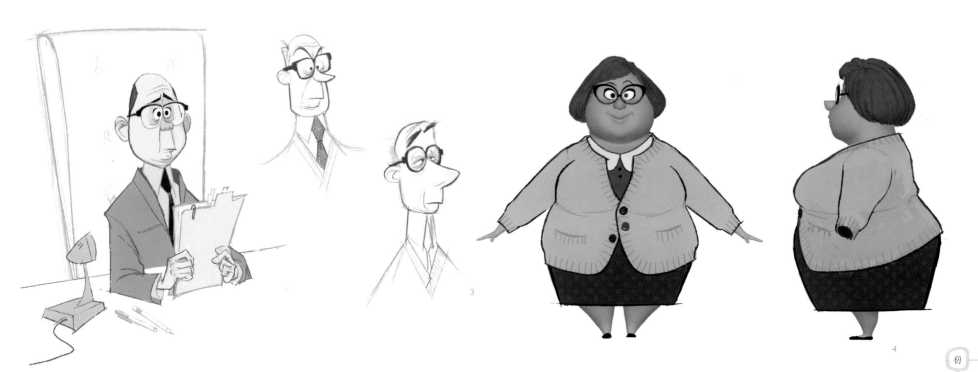

3

4

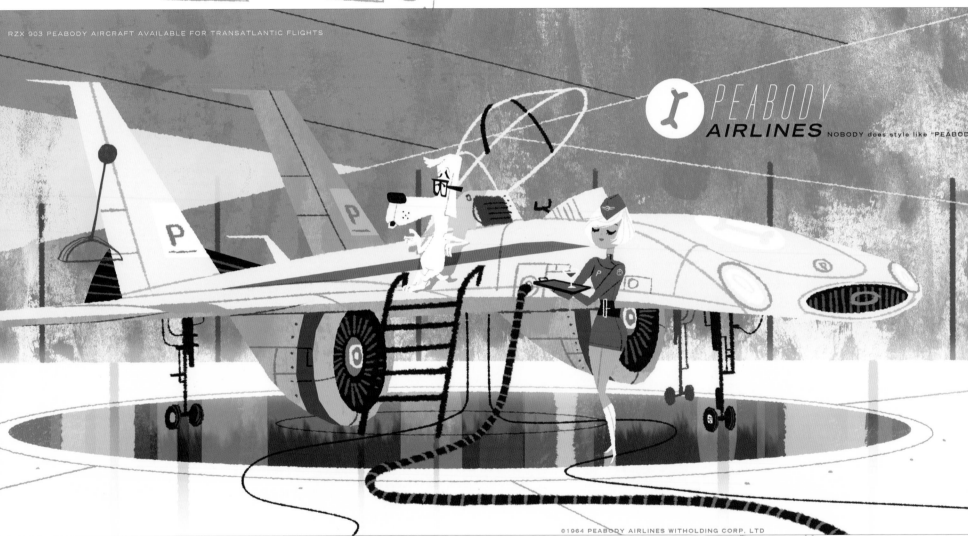

PEABODY
AIRLINES NOBODY does style like "PEABODY"

THESE PAGES • KEVIN DART

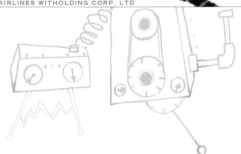

KEVIN DART POSTERS

During the initial visual development process, production designer David James enlisted artist Kevin Dart to create a group of retro-Peabody poster images to help set the proper tone. "We do an internal branding process, which says to our artists, 'Hey, this is the vibe of our film,'" says James. "It's a quick way to get people to think in the style of the movie, to get our artists talking."

As Mr. Peabody was a creation of the late 1950s and early 1960s *Mad Men* era, Dart created several pieces in the style of the advertising art from that time. "Kevin's work is super-evocative of that period," says James. "You just look at it and there's a lot of fun there."

The posters, hung at DreamWorks in both Glendale and Redwood City for inspiration, put the animators in the right frame of mind to tackle an update of a classic. The art features Peabody immersed in his sophisticated, jet-set lifestyle, surrounded by high-tech transportation and fashionable ladies, usually with a cocktail in his hand. "I wanted to shed more light on Mr. Peabody's debonair nature," notes James. Clearly these reflect his earlier days before adopting Sherman and committing himself to raising a child.

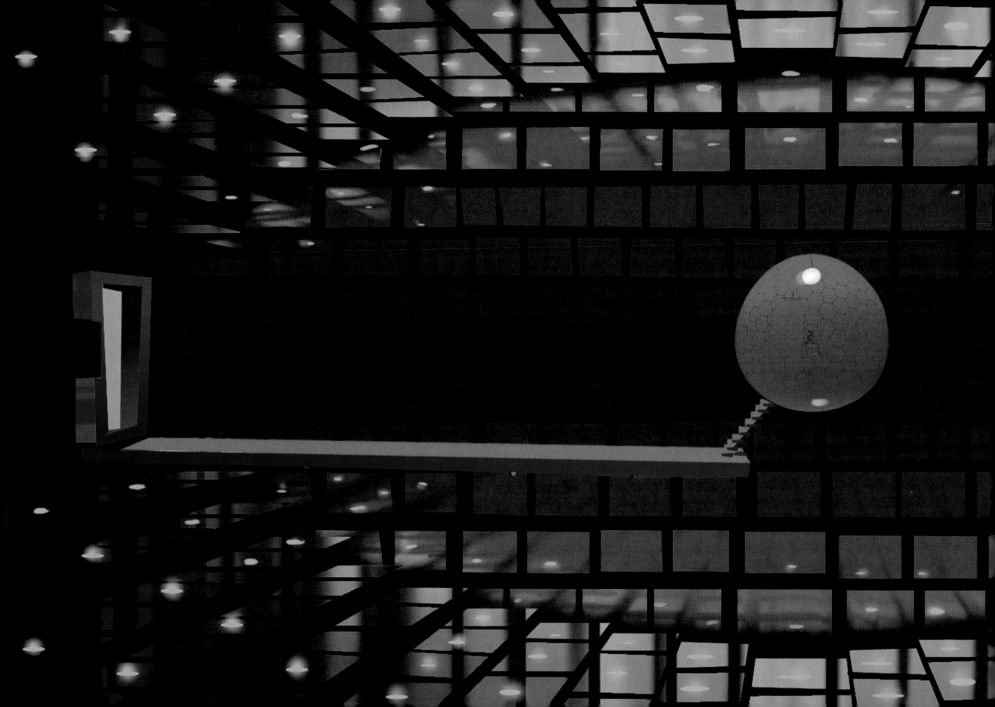

THE WABAC MACHINE

There is a third important member of the Peabody family. No, it's not a person or a pet, but it lives under the same roof. It's the scientific marvel that allows Mr. Peabody & Sherman to visit the past: the WABAC Machine.

Its name (riffing off the 1950s UNIVAC computer) stands for "Way Back," which is how it's pronounced. "The WABAC Machine, as we knew it in the original Jay Ward cartoons, was a door that one simply walked through, and you'd find yourself in the midst of history," says production designer David James. "We loved this idea and struggled long and hard to try to incorporate the door into the aesthetic of the WABAC Machine. For narrative reasons, though, we needed a vehicle—a time-traveling vehicle."

After various concepts were created for a vehicular WABAC Machine, the final design is itself a very simple shape: round.

The classic "red door" is still the portal to the past, but this time it functions as the barrier between the laboratory and a WABAC Machine holding room, loosely inspired by a San Francisco–area sound-experience theater. "There is this place there called Audium, which is one of your weirder cultural artifact leftovers from the 1970s," says James. "There are these amazing fabric panels that are

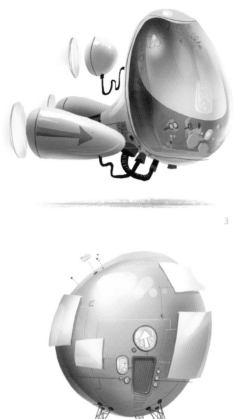

3

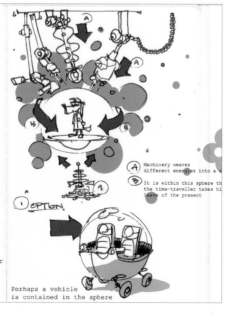

4

5

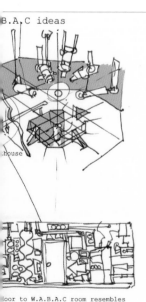

.B.A.C ideas

house

oor to W.A.B.A.C room resembles
riginal cartoon

LARGE HADRON COLLIDER

W.A.B.A.C room contains elaborate machinery
all focused on a central point. The floor
of the room looks like the Large Hadron Collider
at CERN.

Ⓐ Machinery weaves
different energies into a

Ⓑ It is within this sphere th
the time-traveller takes hi
leave of the present

① OPTION

Perhaps a vehicle
is contained in the sphere

6

1–4 • TIM LAMB

5 • SHANE PRIGMORE

6 • DAVID JAMES

suspended from the ceiling, and multiple speakers in this bizarre symmetrical ring. The effect of these floating square panels is very, very science fiction. Quite inspirational."

After visiting Audium, James asked visual development artist Alex Puvilland to check it out too. He then came up with the idea of using reflecting mirrors to convey the idea of space repeating into infinity and the way light travels back and forth. Mirror effects and unlimited reflection posed a technical challenge, but it was a perfect metaphor for time travel and the ability to peer into endless space.

"It gave a very, very interesting aesthetic in what is also a very, very clean-looking room," says James. "There are no wires; everything is concealed. It's more mysterious to not reveal the inner workings." The personality of Mr. Peabody himself loans itself to the clean aesthetic. "He is a clean dog," notes James.

Also, if you look closely, you'll note that in several places in the room, there are echoes of great and some not-so-great science fiction films. That's quite appropriate, as the ranks of classic science fiction icons can now count a few new members: Mr. Peabody, Sherman, and the WABAC Machine.

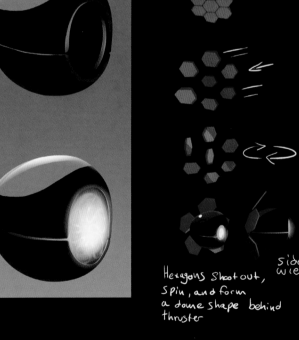

Version I

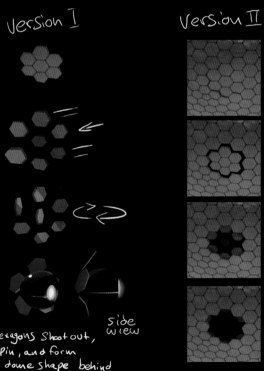

Hexagons shoot out,
spin, and form
a dome shape behind
thruster

side
view

Version II

Hexagons detach from
each other, pushing inwards
and slide behind the
window that is formed in the
WABAC

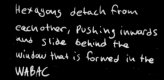

FLOATING PARTS

Peabody and Sherman

WABAC MACHINE!

MOVING ELEMENTS

BOUNCING BALLS

"DELICATE" LANDING
UNBALANCED LANDING GEAR

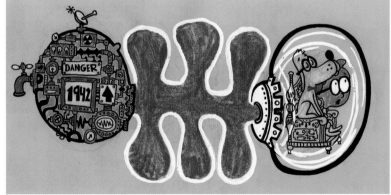

DANGER
1942

1 • DAVID JAMES

2 • AVNER GELLER

3 • ALEX PUVILLAND

4 • JJ VILLARD

5 • DAVID JAMES

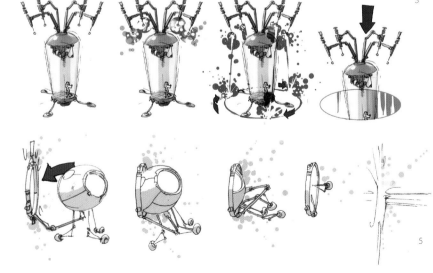

3

4

5

1, 2 • ALEX PUVILLAND

3, 4 • ROBIN JOSEPH

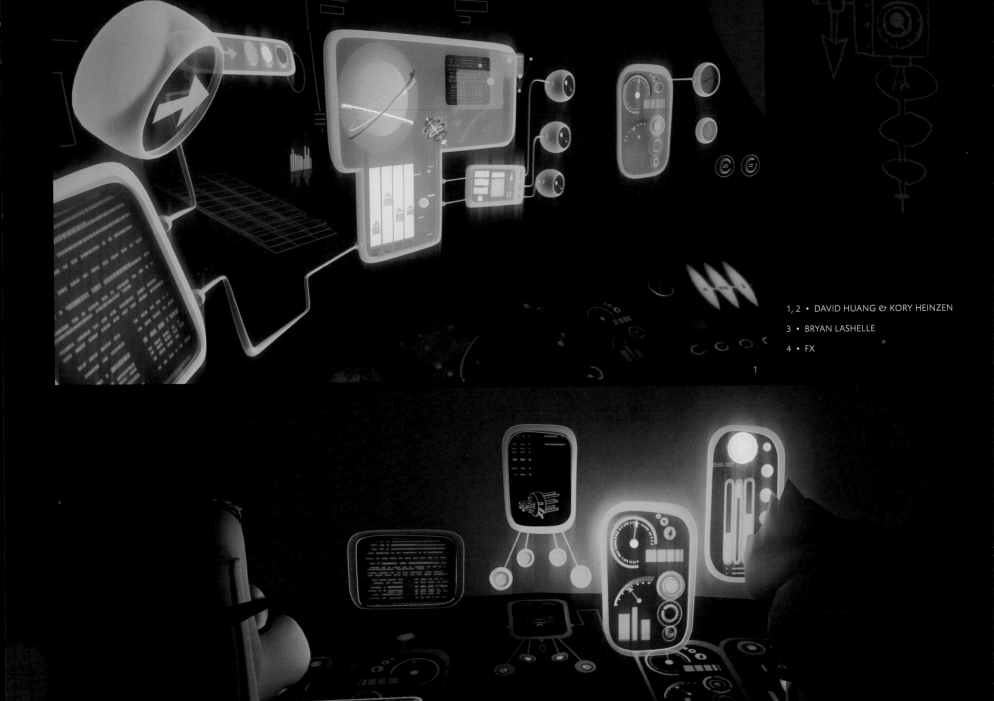

1, 2 • DAVID HUANG & KORY HEINZEN

3 • BRYAN LASHELLE

4 • FX

1

2

PEABODY'S TRAVELS

TIME TRAVEL

Time travel is a fantasy for most of us, something that exists only in the realm of science fiction. However, if you happen to be Mr. Peabody, all you need to do is set the time and place on the WABAC Machine, and you're off to visit any era you desire! Journeys to the past were a staple of the original Jay Ward series, and this movie continues the legacy. With all of history to choose from, DreamWorks Animation chief creative officer Bill Damaschke recalls that the production team had to exercise caution: "We had to figure out how to create a personal story between the two characters and not let the gimmick of time travel overwhelm it."

"In every version of the story," director Rob Minkoff relates, "we were always planning to have Mr. Peabody & Sherman go on time-travel adventures and meet a variety of characters. We went through so many possibilities, concepts, and ideas, because there's an infinite number of places to go and people to meet.

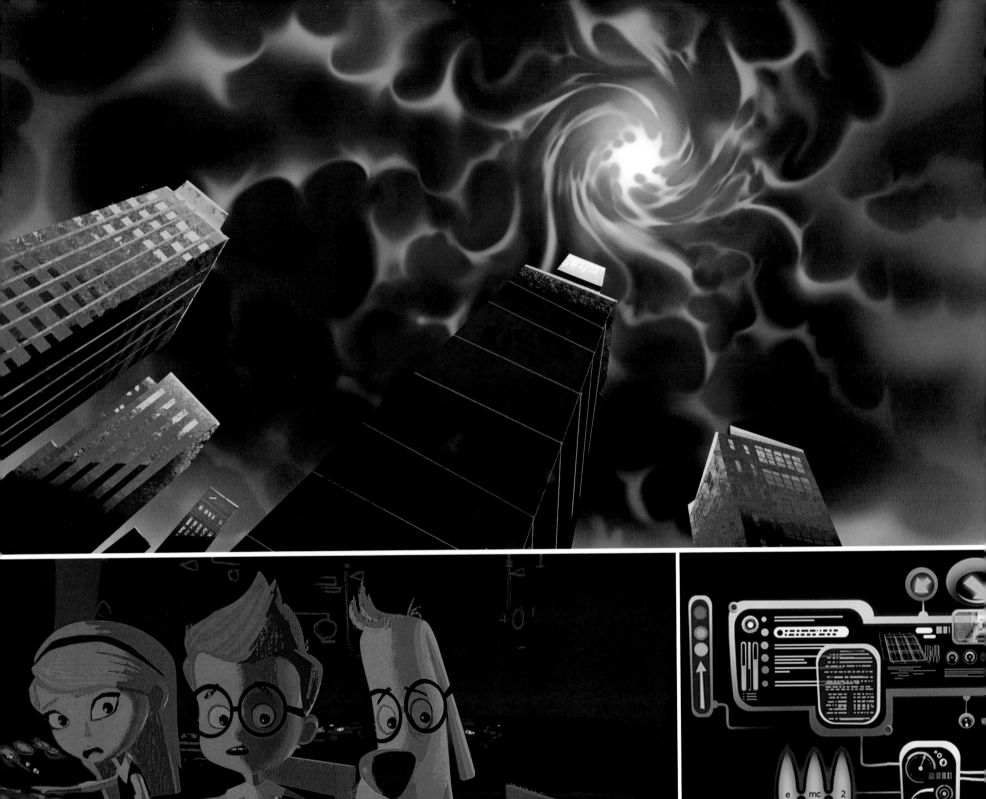

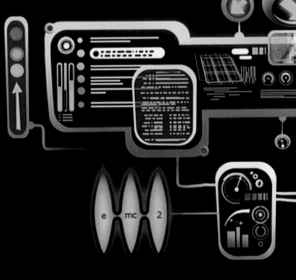

3

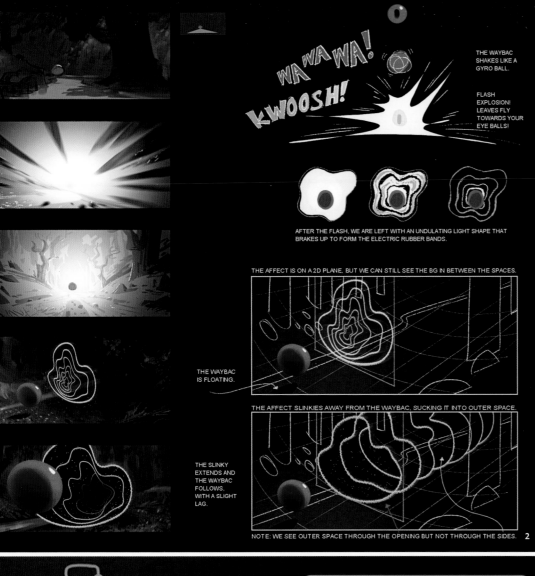

WA WA WA!

KWOOSH!

THE WAYBAC SHAKES LIKE A GYRO BALL.

FLASH EXPLOSION! LEAVES FLY TOWARDS YOUR EYE BALLS!

AFTER THE FLASH, WE ARE LEFT WITH AN UNDULATING LIGHT SHAPE THAT BRAKES UP TO FORM THE ELECTRIC RUBBER BANDS.

THE AFFECT IS ON A 2D PLANE, BUT WE CAN STILL SEE THE BG IN BETWEEN THE SPACES.

THE WAYBAC IS FLOATING.

THE AFFECT SLINKIES AWAY FROM THE WAYBAC, SUCKING IT INTO OUTER SPACE.

THE SLINKY EXTENDS AND THE WAYBAC FOLLOWS, WITH A SLIGHT LAG.

NOTE: WE SEE OUTER SPACE THROUGH THE OPENING BUT NOT THROUGH THE SIDES. 2

796973911020

1964 AD

SYSTEMS
INTERFACE
INFO
time

4

5

Narrowing it down was a bit of a challenge." Minkoff knew that a key task would be deciding exactly whom Mr. Peabody & Sherman would meet up with: "We had lists of characters, a cross section of historical figures that had to be remarkable enough that people would know who they are. There's a whole set of people that would be known in America but perhaps not outside America. We needed characters who would be recognizable to a broad swath of people."

Head of story Walt Dohrn remembers enjoying the exploration. "We had a lot of fun pushing these ideas," he says, "figuring how far we could go without being ridiculous or disrespectful. Who is Marie Antoinette? We had all kinds of crazy characterizations for King Tut. We ended up pushing and pulling them in interesting ways: Does Agamemnon have a Greek accent, or is he like a frat guy or a jock?"

Not all the characters Mr. Peabody & Sherman meet are famous. Producer Alex Schwartz recalls one of her favorites: "Odysseus wasn't originally a character in the movie, but we needed to name one of the Greek soldiers and decided to assign him that identity. His character design and animation was so funny that we started looking for more

1 • PRISCILLA WONG   4 • KORY HEINZEN

2 • RUBEN PEREZ   5 • TIM LAMB

3 • BRYAN LASHELLE

 "Each time period needed a distinct look, since the film is visually episodic. Each historical period will tend to skew to a certain type of design caricature."

DAVID JAMES,
PRODUCTION DESIGNER

2

1 • RUBEN PEREZ   3 • KEN PAK

2 • CARLOS FELIPE LEÓN   4 • AVNER GELLER

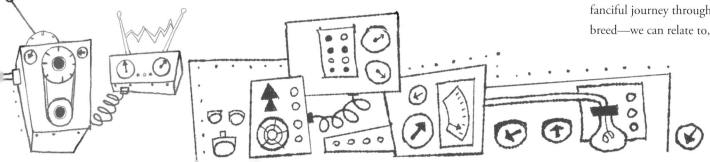

places to put him in the movie. Small bit of trivia: He is voiced by DreamWorks Animation director Tom McGrath, who also voices Skipper the Penguin in *Madagascar*."

Character designer Joe Moshier and art director Tim Lamb had free reign to create visuals for these great figures in history. Lamb has vivid memories of Moshier's approach: "When we did Napoleon, he drew him as a tiny round ball of a guy, maybe three feet tall, with a hat that extended his body length. He would take original oil paintings of Napoleon and boil it down to the funniest versions of him. He did that with all the characters."

Peabody's travels and improbable history were a balancing act for the production team, who needed to include elements of time travel beside the unique story of a dog who adopted a boy and their relationship.

By their nature, time-travel stories can become rather convoluted, so developing a final script posed its own challenges. Schwartz notes: "Our screenwriter Craig Wright pushed it in a direction that had real emotional resonance and simple truth: parents and children struggle, and children eventually grow up."

Even with the time travel in play, Minkoff agrees that the story ultimately became about the shifting family dynamic: "The story of a father and a son, and a son that's growing up. That's really the theme I think Craig wanted to explore, about how time affects everything and all of us."

With the story and characters jelling, it was up to production designer David James to structure a fantastic yet believable past for our heroes to visit. "Each time period needed a distinct look, since the film is visually episodic," he says. "Each historical period will tend to skew to a certain type of design caricature. Take the impossible verticality of Troy: It exists in the popular imagination as a wall that can't be scaled. So Troy in our movie is so exaggerated, so extreme in size, you can barely see the top of the wall. It's much like human caricature; if a person has a big nose, that's what you're going to exaggerate. So, what is the 'big nose' of each historical period?"

Before Mr. Peabody & Sherman stepped into the WABAC machine, many talented and imaginative people collaborated in planning their travels and adventures. The result of their effort is a fanciful journey through time with characters—no matter what their breed—we can relate to, laugh with, and believe in. Let's get going!

BRYAN LASHELLE

FRENCH REVOLUTION

The film begins in the ornate, pristine palace of Marie Antoinette. David James, the production designer, had definite ideas on how the queen's banquet should look and feel. "Marie Antoinette's world is entirely pastel, very low contrast and very refined," he says. "We create visual interest by using the color accent of the giant pink cake." The cake in question becomes the object of Sherman's desire and the catalyst of the French Revolution.

Once the revolution begins, the color palette shifts accordingly. "On the other hand," recalls James, "when you go onto the Place de la Concorde, with the guillotine, and all through the Paris sewers, we basically go to black-and-white imagery—except in this case, it is black with dramatic reds, oranges, and brown tones."

1, 3 • ALEX PUVILLAND

2 • RUBEN PEREZ

1 • PASCAL CAMPION

2 • KEN PAK

3 • KORY HEINZEN

"When you go onto the Place de la Concorde, with the guillotine, and all through the Paris sewers, we basically go to black-and-white imagery—except in this case, it is black with dramatic reds, oranges, and brown tones."

DAVID JAMES, PRODUCTION DESIGNER

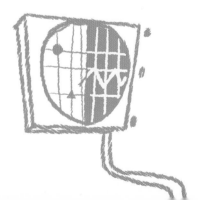

2

3

"It is basically red-and-white imagery. Very, very dramatic, hopefully to the point that people realize this is a bit over the top."

DAVID JAMES,
PRODUCTION DESIGNER

Marie Antoinette

"Marie Antoinette's world is entirely pastel, very low contrast and very refined. We create visual interest by using the color accent of the giant pink cake."

DAVID JAMES, PRODUCTION DESIGNER

1, 3 • JOE MOSHIER   5, 6 • PRISCILLA WONG
2, 4 • TIM LAMB   7 • KEN PAK

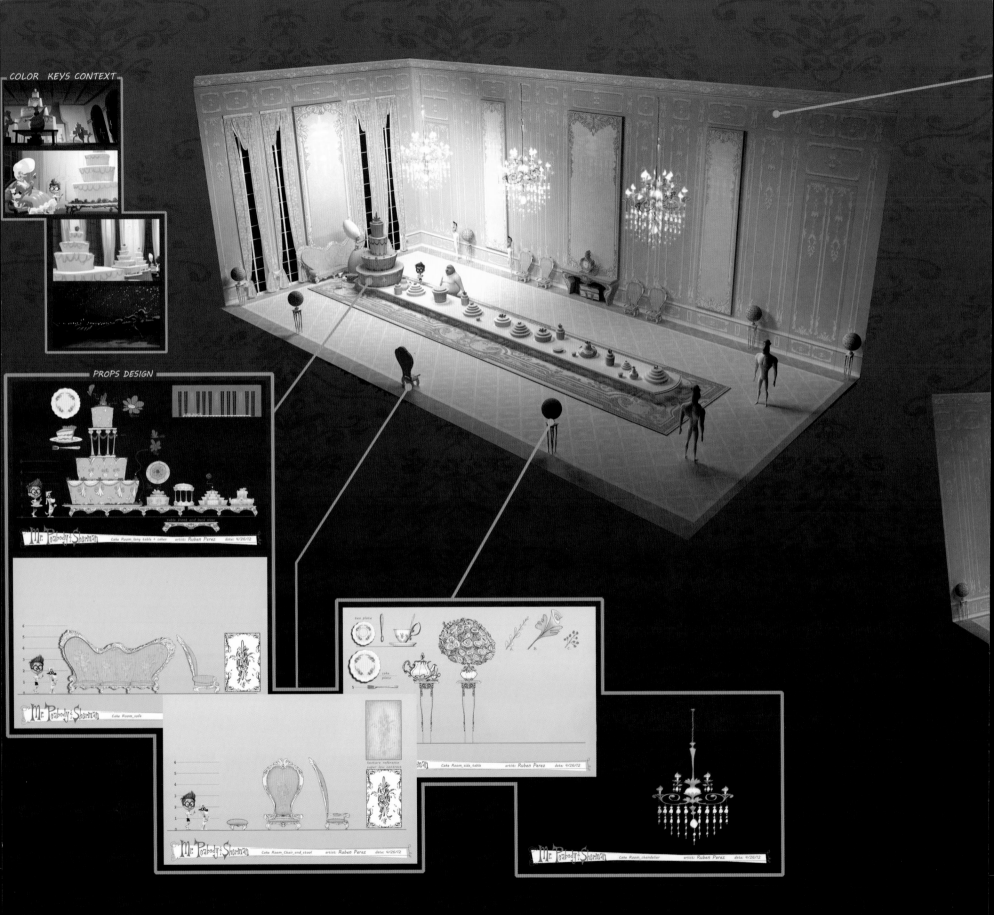

COLOR KEYS CONTEXT

PROPS DESIGN

THESE PAGES • RUBEN PEREZ

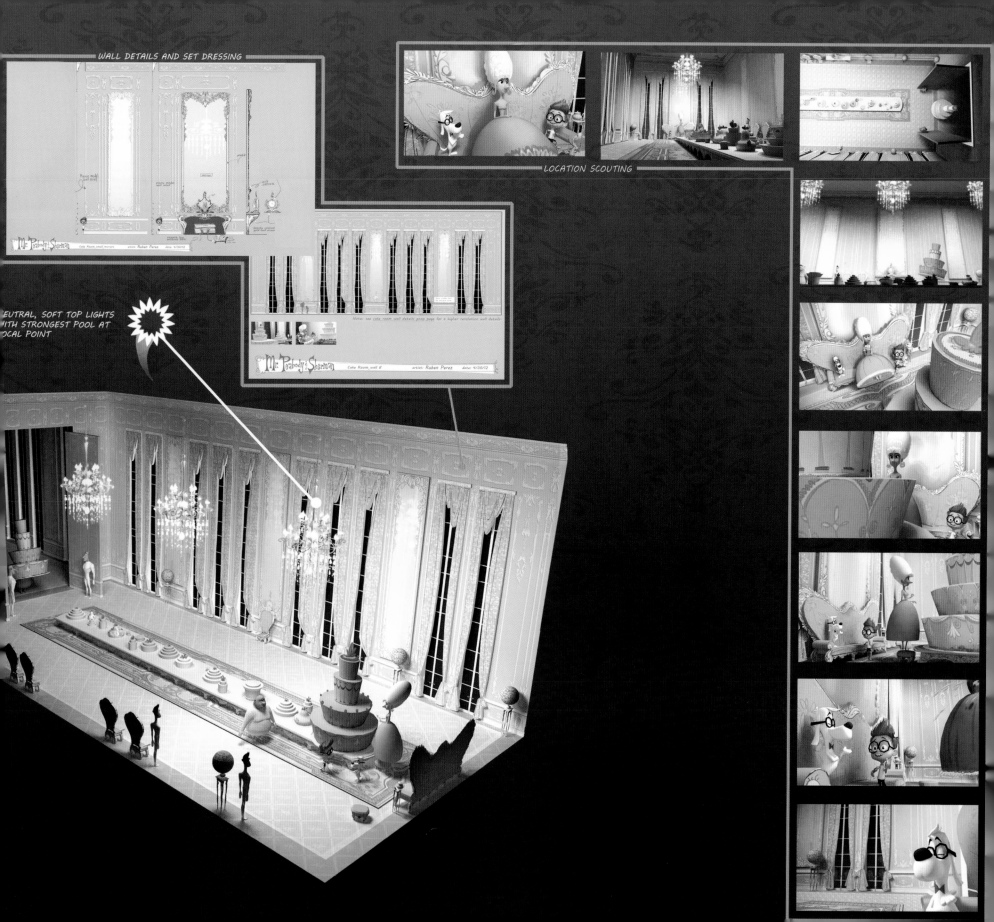

WALL DETAILS AND SET DRESSING

LOCATION SCOUTING

NEUTRAL, SOFT TOP LIGHTS
WITH STRONGEST POOL AT
FOCAL POINT

EGYPT

ncient tombs, the Sphinx, holy temples, sacred ceremonies . . . all in a day's work (a day in 1332 B.C.) for Mr. Peabody & Sherman as they attempt to rescue Penny from a fate worse than death: marriage to King Tut! Obstacles abound, all of them delightfully conceived in production paintings by visual development artists Ken Pak, Kory Heinzen, and Ruben Perez.

Penny has used the WABAC Machine to do what many a young girl might do if given half a chance: become a princess. In this case, Princess Hatshepsut, aka "precious flower of the Nile." Her new boyfriend is a young King Tut, and they are set to be married—and mummified, unless Mr. Peabody & Sherman can escape a sealed tomb.

"In Egypt, we used several distinct palettes," recalls production designer David James. "The first is when we meet Penny by the pool, eating almonds and honey, a little bit of a Liz Taylor–Cleopatra vibe there, bathed in an exotic light. Then there is the second part, the 'Tomb Escape,' done in an old adventure serial style, with dark alleys and torch-lit corridors but, of course, slightly slapstick and comedic. And then there is the wedding, an even more dramatic environment, bleached out, very brightly lit."

To heighten the suspense, the images of Egypt were the most naturalistic in the film. But that didn't mean the artists couldn't have a little fun with the settings. "On our first DreamWorks animated feature, *The Prince of Egypt*, we had a no 'Easter Egg' policy— especially no gags or in-jokes on the hieroglyphics," confesses James. "We'd been waiting for years to do this. If you look close at the hieroglyphs in the tomb sequence, all of them are little gags. Each one a joke. Literally wall-to-wall."

1 • KEN PAK

2 • RUBEN PEREZ

King Tut

1 • CARLOS FELIPE LEÓN

2, 6 • TIM LAMB

3–5 • ZAC WOLLONS

7 • KEN PAK

Cleopatra

1 • JOE MOSHIER

2 • TIM LAMB, RUBEN PEREZ & KORY HEINZEN

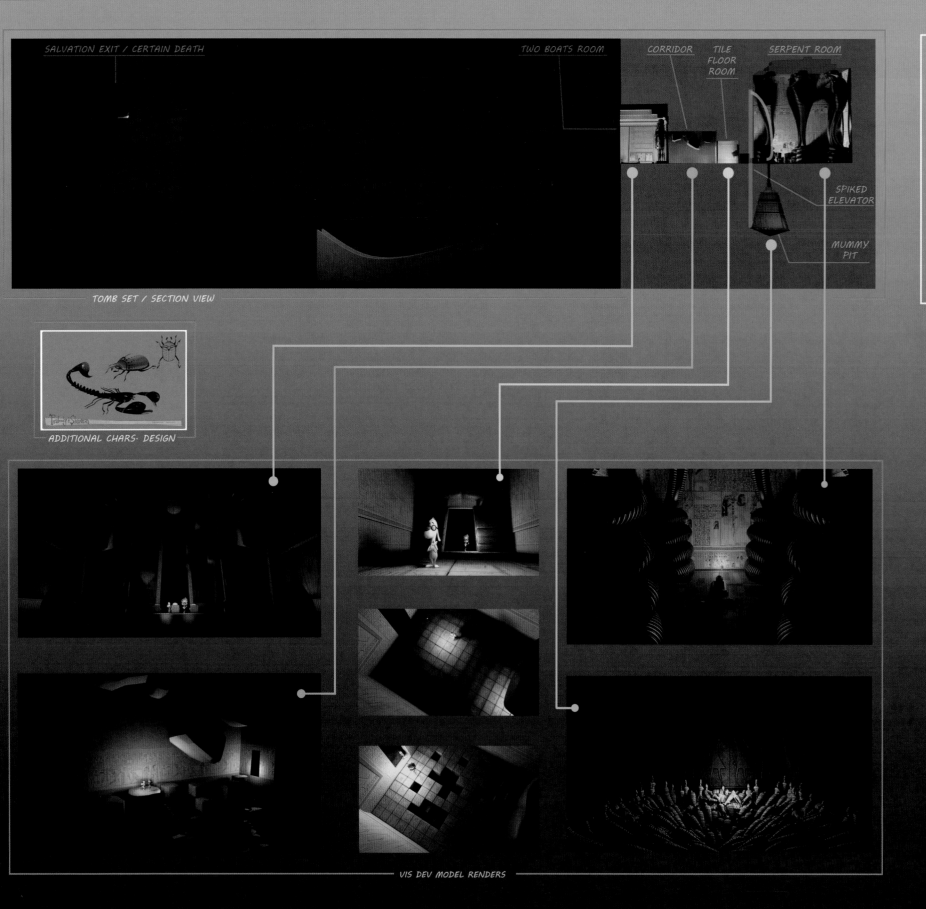

SALVATION EXIT / CERTAIN DEATH

TWO BOATS ROOM

CORRIDOR

TILE FLOOR ROOM

SERPENT ROOM

SPIKED ELEVATOR

MUMMY PIT

TOMB SET / SECTION VIEW

ADDITIONAL CHARS· DESIGN

VIS DEV MODEL RENDERS

THESE PAGES • CARLOS ZARAGOZA, RUBEN PEREZ & DAVID HUANG

COLOR KEYS / SERPENT ROOM

COLOR KEYS — TILE ROOM TO BOATS

CEILING TRAP DOOR

SPIKED ELEVATOR

SLIDE
[BACK TO
SERPENT ROOM]

LIGHTING
TORCH LIGHTS
CARRIED BY
CHARACTERS

WALL OF HIEROGLYPHS

HIDDEN DOOR

SERPENT ROOM

BOAT
SLIDE

CORRIDOR

TILE FLOOR
ROOM

FLOOR TRAP DOOR
[TO PIT]

COLOR KEYS

TWO BOATS ROOM

MUMMY
PIT

TRAP DOOR

MUMMY PIT

RIOR / VIS DEV MODEL / SCHEMATIC VIEW [SERPENT TO BOATS ROOM SECTION]

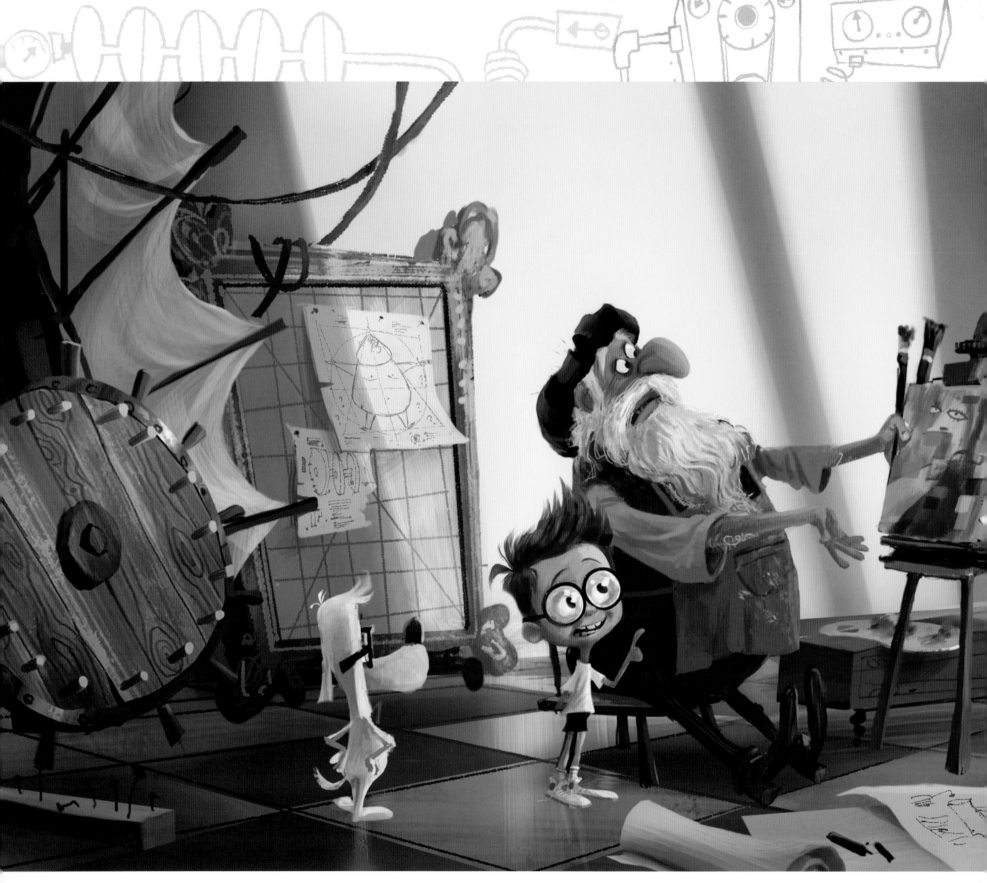

TIM LAMB

FLORENCE

A visit to the Italian countryside, and to Leonardo da Vinci's workshop, is played both for laughs and as a relaxing pit stop between Egyptian sacrifices and black holes. "The idea was to use Florence as it exists in the background of Renaissance paintings, with exaggerated palettes," notes production designer David James. "The Duomo in our world is impossibly huge. We tried to move away from a perfectly modular system to something broader, swerving, and much wilder."

Jason Schleifer, head of character animation, worked with his team to explore da Vinci himself—a historical character who almost steals the show. "Supervising animator Jason Spencer-Galsworthy and his team really had fun with da Vinci," he recalls. "He's a crazy old man—passionate, with lots of energy. We wanted to make him fun, so from the moment the audience sees him they think, 'Oh, I really like this guy!' It's the same with Mona Lisa; she is very stylized and her actions are pushed to an extreme."

"The idea was to use Florence as it exists in the background of Renaissance paintings, with exaggerated palettes."

DAVID JAMES,
PRODUCTION DESIGNER

Leonardo da Vinci

"We wanted to make [da Vinci] fun, so from the moment the audience sees him they think, 'Oh, I really like this guy!'"

JASON SCHLEIFER, HEAD OF CHARACTER ANIMATION

1, 2 • JOE MOSHIER

3 • TIM LAMB

4

Mona Lisa

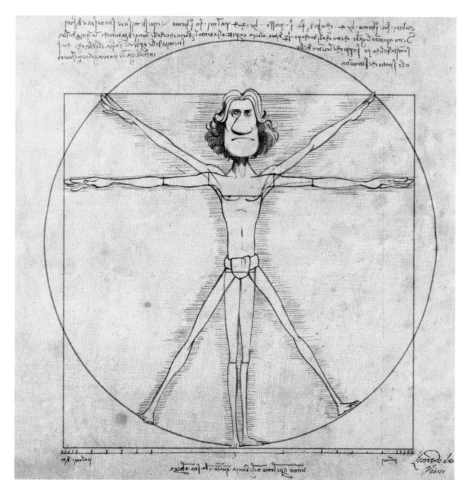

5

4 • BRYAN LASHELLE

5 • TIM LAMB

6 • CARLOS FELIPE LEÓN

6

1, 3 • BRYAN LASHELLE

2 • AVNER GELLER

4 • NIC HENDERSON

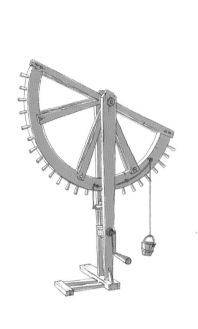

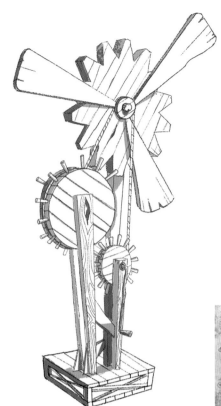

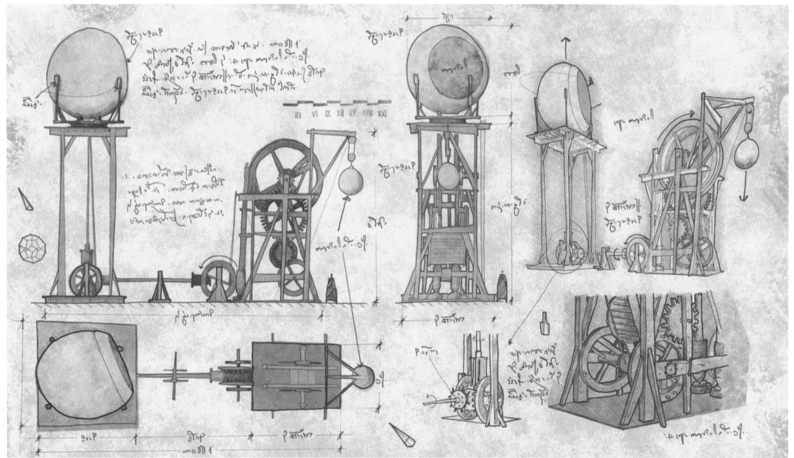

1 • PRISCILLA WONG

2 • KEN PAK

3 • DAVID HUANG & TIM LAMB

1

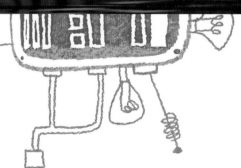

6

TROY

A ncient Troy is on the brink of one of history's most ferocious conflicts, the Trojan War. Shermanus—Sherman's name as a member of the Greek Army—has run off from Mr. Peabody and attempts to prove himself by going to war. This sequence, mainly at night and highly dramatic, has its share of comedic moments, mostly around the designs and personalities of the Greeks and the look of the famed Trojan Horse.

"There's some speculation as to where Troy was, what it actually looked like," says production designer David James. "The Trojan Horse is more of a story than historical fact. There are drawings, some carvings. There's the notion that Troy is a walled city that looks like a birthday cake that goes higher and higher. What Troy inhabits in our collective imagination is a city behind an impassible wall. In the film, our first glimpse of Troy is of this massive horse, and we deliberately designed the city to dwarf the horse. Troy became a monolithic thing there was no getting around."

> "What Troy inhabits in our collective imagination is a city behind an impassible wall. In the film . . . Troy became a monolithic thing there was no getting around."
>
> DAVID JAMES,
> PRODUCTION DESIGNER

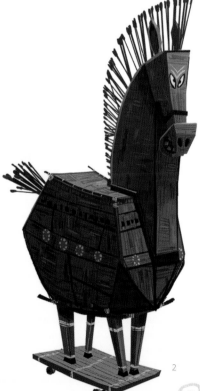

1

1 • KEN PAK

2 • BRYAN LASHELLE

2

121

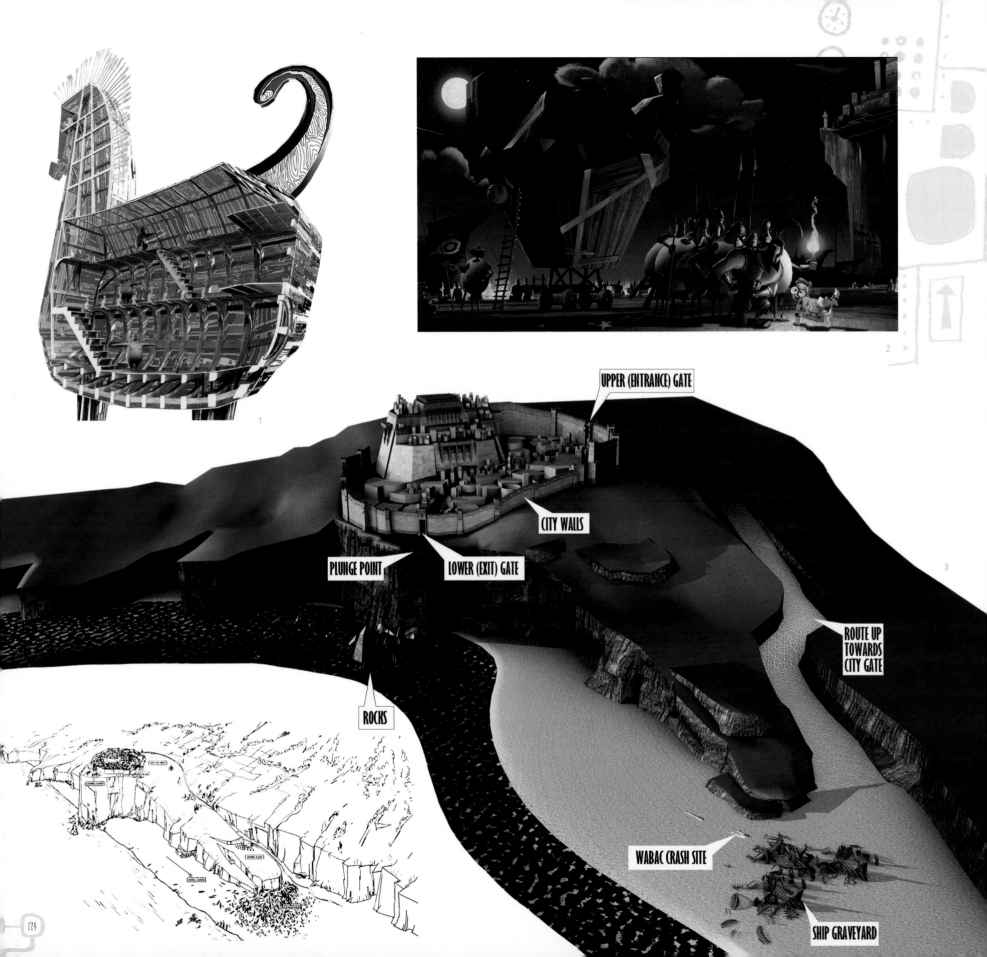

UPPER (ENTRANCE) GATE

CITY WALLS

PLUNGE POINT

LOWER (EXIT) GATE

ROUTE UP TOWARDS CITY GATE

ROCKS

WABAC CRASH SITE

SHIP GRAVEYARD

"I love shape. I love pushing proportions," says character designer Joe Moshier. "To me, design is design. You're designing to make something look hopefully fresh and appealing." Moshier is a prolific artist who works to the style of the film and the mood of a scene: "It feels like a cartoon; it's a cartoon. They don't use that word much these days, but the further away from the Uncanny Valley, the better. I really do like cartoony CG. That's what *Mr. Peabody & Sherman* is, and I'm going to call it."

1 • NIC HENDERSON, BRYAN LASHELLE & AVNER GELLER

2 • ALEX PUVILLAND

3 • ZAC WOLLONS, NIC HENDERSON & RUBEN PEREZ

4 • NIC HENDERSON

5 • KEN PAK

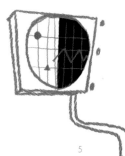

"I love shape. I love pushing proportions. To me, design is design. You're designing to make something look hopefully fresh and appealing."

JOE MOSHIER, CHARACTER DESIGNER

Agamemnon and Odysseus

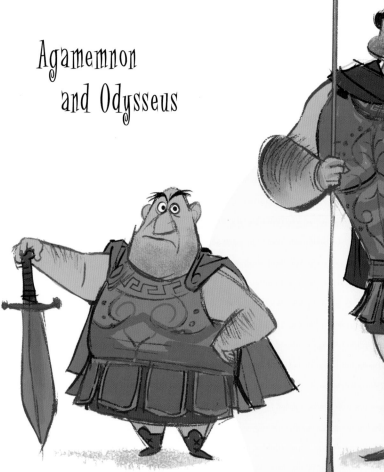

"The world Jay Ward created was so cartoonish and crazy that we had a very interesting fine line to walk. We wanted our historical figures to be recognizable without being overly realistic."

DAVID JAMES,
PRODUCTION DESIGNER

GALLERY OF HISTORIC FIGURES

There were literally dozens of historic figures considered for a part in *Mr. Peabody & Sherman*—some of them make cameos throughout the film or during the end credits. Others were simply left on the drawing board. Art director Tim Lamb headed the design team, aided by visual development artists and character designers. "We began by establishing a shape and design language with our main characters Mr. Peabody & Sherman," explains Lamb. "That's your first flag in the ground—and once we established that, every set and location in the film was designed to complement and support the playful quality of the characters."

Joe Moshier had a ball with the idea of coming up with historical characters that all had to fit into Peabody's world: "Historical characters? It's really just an exercise in caricature. I didn't look at other people's caricatures of these iconic characters or people. I wanted to give my take on these big figures in history, and, hopefully, try to give a fresh perspective." Joe Moshier took the lead on the characters of Gandhi and Confucius, who was his favorite character of all because of the dramatic proportions. It allowed him to focus on tiny features in the middle of an extremely large face. Moshier's background in animation was a boon in helping these outlandish characters still feel believable and alive.

"There are so many incredibly talented character designers out there today," says Tim Lamb, "but Joe Moshier has this extra ability to reference a real character in history and capture that character's likeness and find a way to make it funny or clever. He is a character designer who has a special gift in caricaturing."

11

12

13

14

15

1 • PRISCILLA WONG   7, 8 • TIM LAMB

2, 4–6, 12–15 • JOE MOSHIER   9 • SHANE PRIGMORE

3 • CRAIG KELLMAN   10, 11 • SHANNON TINDLE

5

8

6

7

9

Places Not Traveled

1 • PASCAL CAMPION

2 • TIM LAMB

3, 4 • PRISCILLA WONG

3

4

1 • SHANE PRIGMORE

2, 3 • TIM LAMB

4 • NATE WRAGG

BUILDING A SCENE

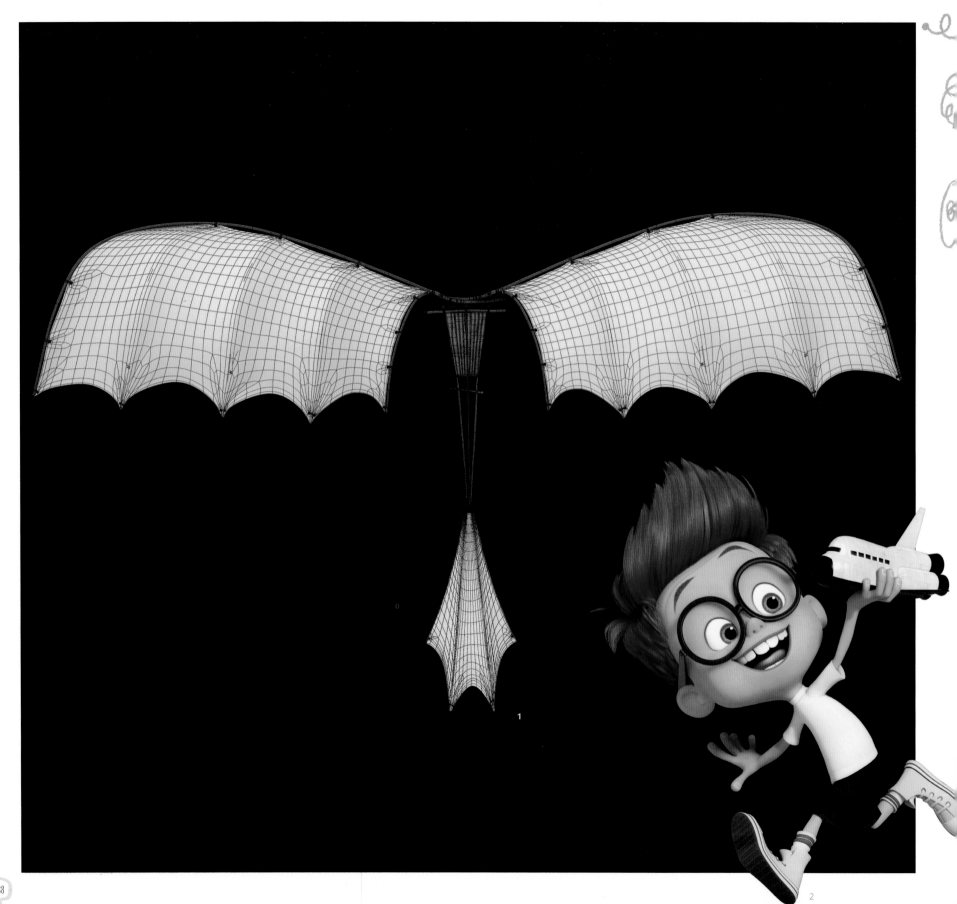

SEQUENCE 1680

THE FLYING MACHINE

SHERMAN: Wow, Mr. Peabody, that was pretty fantastic! But how did they make such a great movie about it? It must have been really hard!

MR. PEABODY: Not at all, Sherman. The geniuses at DreamWorks Animation—second only to me, of course—knew how to break down the job one step at a time. They, too, knew Rome wasn't built in a day. And speaking of Rome, perhaps I can illustrate how their work is done by examining one of my very favorite scenes in the picture, our journey to the time of Leonardo da Vinci. Recall, Sherman, the marvelous vistas, the matchless beauty of the Italian countryside, the historic architecture, the rustic atmosphere—

SHERMAN: The crashing of Mr. da Vinci's flying machine into a tree!

MR. PEABODY: Ah . . . yes, I'm afraid you did do that. However, there was much more to it than you and Penny having an aerial misadventure. In order to create the scene—number 1680 to be exact—technicians, writers, animators, and artists planned for months. For each second we were on the screen, hundreds of hours of work went into convincing audiences that you, Penny, Mr. da Vinci, and I were there before their very eyes. If one hair on your head were out of place, Sherman, they would have corrected it. Not only that, these same artists had to depict Mr. da Vinci's world down to the smallest detail.

SHERMAN: I wouldn't even know where to start.

MR. PEABODY: Precisely, Sherman. That is why no individual could have produced this scene on his or her own. It takes an entire team, each person having their own area of expertise. First, there are writers who develop and shape the script. Designers and artists determine the ambience of Sequence 1680. Experts in modeling and surfacing give our flying machine shape and texture. Animators, using the latest technology, design the four of us on their computers and calculate our slightest movements in a process called "rigging." Specialists in lighting contribute realism, and the visual effects team lends the scene a special touch by contributing details such as the splashes of water when you and Penny frolick over the river.

SHERMAN: And they all have to work together, right, Mr. Peabody?

MR. PEABODY: Exactly, my boy. Collaboration and teamwork are the keys to success. Now, if you're ready, let's revisit Sequence 1680 for a complete examination of how it was done.

1 • PEABODY MODELING

2, 4 • PEABODY PRODUCTION

3 • PEABODY SURFACING

4

Story and Layout

MR. PEABODY: Of course, the scene we are discussing is part of a story. Although you would naturally expect there to be a script, the DreamWorks team expands on it through a process that amazes even me—it's called pre-vis, or previsualization.

SHERMAN: You mean, like being able to see ahead?

MR. PEABODY: More than that, Sherman. As the head of layout, Mr. Kent Seki, explained to me, it's a primitive working version of the scene, including how each camera angle is set up, how the backgrounds will look, the use of lighting, and how the characters and other objects will move through the scene. It is, in fact, a cinematic storyboard that serves to set the appearance and actions of every aspect of what happened when we paid our visit to Leonardo da Vinci. If all goes well, there is not much difference between what is previsualized and what reaches the screen.

SHERMAN: So that's how they plan out the whole scene, right?

MR. PEABODY: You're close, my boy. The animatics—that is, the actions that will take place in the scene—are reviewed by the director, the lighting and effects experts, and the film editor. If changes are required, they can be done at this stage, ensuring that no time and efforts are wasted when it comes to the final shoot. It is an ongoing, collaborative process. Here, have a look.

SHERMAN: But, Mr. Peabody, that doesn't look like you.

MR. PEABODY: Not to worry, Sherman. The animator—that is, the artist who finalizes our appearances and movements—is able to place the previsualization into his own computer and animate directly over the rough animatics, producing the strikingly handsome dog you observed in the film. The same goes for Mr. da Vinci, his marvelous inventions, and even the Mona Lisa. They made only one error I was able to detect.

SHERMAN: Really, Mr. Peabody?

MR. PEABODY: Yes, Sherman. Allowing you up in the flying machine in the first place.

Visual Development

SHERMAN: Mr. Peabody, how did the DreamWorks artists know what da Vinci's Italy looked like? Do they have a WABAC Machine like ours?

MR. PEABODY: They used a mixture of diligent study and imagination, Sherman. I was able to observe production designer David James poring over this very problem. He began with the idea that each distinct locale we visited had its own look and style. From there, he honed in on Renaissance paintings depicting Florence. However, Mr. James aimed to caricature, rather than make an exact copy of, the city where Leonardo da Vinci lived. In fact, Sherman, do you realize that the Duomo you managed to fly Mr. da Vinci's contraption through was so enlarged in scale that the windows would have been thirty-four feet high?

SHERMAN: Good thing, Mr. Peabody! Penny and I barely made it through as it was!

MR. PEABODY: Quite. As Mr. James put it, the challenge was deciding which feature of a given time period was most amenable to caricature. In the case of Florence, it was the dominating architecture. You may be interested to know, Sherman, that the same process was applied to us. You see, our original appearances as seen on television simply would not do in a scene such as this. You can thank Mr. James for redesigning us to reflect the tremendous advances animation has made since we first appeared in 1959. Where we once lived in a world of two dimensions, we can now inhabit three thanks to the artists of DreamWorks. Yet, our original designs were respected to the point where I remained my urbane, sophisticated self, and you . . . well, you are still very much Sherman.

SHERMAN: It's like using the WABAC Machine to go to the future!

MR. PEABODY: Speaking of the WABAC Machine, I suppose you've noticed that even it is no longer the simple door we once walked through. That's only one of many handsome redesigns by Mr. James and his artists. I admit, however, that I had considerable say in the remodeling of my apartment.

Modeling and Surfacing

SHERMAN: *How do the characters and props turn from hand drawings into dimensional objects that look so real?*

MR. PEABODY: Excellent question, Sherman. Head of modeling Tony Williams and his team, using Maya and proprietary software created at DreamWorks, construct the world of da Vinci's Italy within the computer. Following design rules set by the production designer David James, the crew set about establishing three-dimensional sculptures for the characters, sets, and props required for each scene. For this flying sequence, the team worked for sixty-five weeks, building 224 models for the environment—representing da Vinci's backyard and launch pad, his loft as well as the city of Florence and the surrounding countryside—and seventy-eight props for da Vinci's inventions, set dressing, and various objects.

A surfacing team works with the modeling department to create the realistic surfaces for everything seen on the screen. These artists define the material properties, color, and characteristics of all individual objects—whether they are solid or liquid, hard or soft, from the fifteenth century or the twenty-first. Led by John Wake, the surfacing team constructed the walls, the foliage in the countryside, and even the textures of the wood for the flying machine.

It is particularly challenging in a sequence like this where we had the contrast of legendary personages—such as ourselves and Mr. da Vinci—acting against naturalistic settings. Head of lighting Laura Grieve told me about achieving the right balance.

LAURA GRIEVE: There's this really delicate balance between being too cartoony and too realistic. When you get into scenes, particularly with these kinds of characters, you want them to feel warm and inviting. You can't have the characters feel disconnected from the environments; they need to live in the worlds that we create.

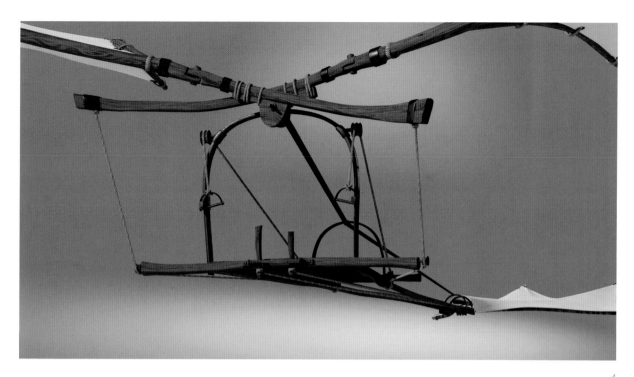

Rigging and Animation

SHERMAN: *But once they sculpt a model in the computer, how do they make it move so realistically?*

MR. PEABODY: That's called "animation," Sherman. The studio is filled with fine artisans known as animators, whose job it is to imbue the illusion of life into the inanimate models created for the film. They provide the acting required for each character and need to be actors themselves in order to provide the appropriate behaviors to imbue each moment with personality.

But before the animators can move the characters and objects, the digital models must be "rigged"—distinct controls are applied by the technical directors so the animators can move them. The more rigging, the more precise the movements and facial expressions. For Sequence 1680, da Vinci's glider had to be specially rigged so the wings could collapse, and so you and Penny could operate the controls.

Another aide for the animators is studying the voice cast. Jason Schleifer, head of character animation, told me that videotaping Max Charles (the boy behind your very voice, Sherman) was vital.

JASON SCHLEIFER: He's amazing. Just the way his mouth moves, the shapes that his face makes as he forms words. Watching him speak was a big influence on us when we were figuring out how to pose Sherman, because he's got big teeth—he's a kid, you know? His mouth shapes are very unique and expressive.

MR. PEABODY: Yes, I know.

SHERMAN: *What's the matter with my teeth?*

MR. PEABODY: Nothing, Sherman! You're a perfectly normal boy with just the right bite!

JASON SCHLEIFER: With Mr. Peabody & Sherman, we want the audience to empathize and recognize themselves in the performances, so we've got to be a little bit more grounded and more believable. We can go crazy and cartoony with them, but they have an arc through the film, so we had to tone it down a little bit and let the audience feel comfortable. Whereas with da Vinci, we just want to make him fun. The moment that the audience sees him, they like him.

MR. PEABODY: They do indeed!

PEABODY MATTE PAINTING

Lighting

SHERMAN: *Ready for your close-up, Mr. Peabody?*

MR. PEABODY: One of the essential finishing touches for each scene is provided by the lighting artists who execute the final look of the film. By combining the proper lighting and shading combinations for every element on screen, these artists help propel the story, convey the drama, or highlight the comedy throughout the film. Working closely with the director, the head of lighting—like a live-action cinematographer—sets the light sources that allow the acting, settings, and situations to be seen clearly and look their best. Head of lighting Laura Grieve uses color keys provided by the art director as a guide to the palette and intensity of the light for each shot.

LAURA GRIEVE: The production designer emphasized to us that Mr. Peabody needed to be the whitest thing in the shot. That was a bit difficult for us. White dogs are really tricky because, if the lighting isn't just so, they can look dirty rather easily or they can look too bright really quickly. White hair behaves really specifically in the way that light scatters through the fine white strands.

SHERMAN: *Especially after he takes a bath!*

MR. PEABODY: Pay attention, Sherman. The lighting work is truly . . . illuminating! I especially appreciate how collaborative it is with the rest of the staff.

LAURA GRIEVE: It is indeed. For example, when we do an initial pass of a sequence, we take a still image from the film and send it to art director Tim Lamb, who does these incredible paint-overs for us. It is much quicker for him to describe something visually on an image than it is for him to describe it verbally. He actually paints over it on a Cintiq tablet. The sequence starts off looking quite rough and then we begin the process of building the look over a number of iterations. The principles of the light direction and light quality, tone, contrast, color, and shadow density are all really well described in Tim's artwork, and it acts as a great starting point for the look of the sequence.

MR. PEABODY: It's like building a painting, but it's based on the physics of light, how light bounces around and how it reflects off other things. The final shot is an actual translation of Tim Lamb's artwork.

Visual Effects

MR. PEABODY: Of course, Sherman, your flight over Florence in Mr. da Vinci's aircraft would not have been convincing at all if it seemed to take place in a vacuum. Luckily, the DreamWorks visual effects team was on hand to provide just the right amount of realism to the scene. Wind and turbulence were essential in convincing the audience that you and Penny were actually affected by your flight conditions. Two units are needed here: CFX, also called character effects; and FX, or visual effects.

SHERMAN: Two? It certainly took a lot of people to get me up in the air and make it look real.

MR. PEABODY: Now, the first unit examines how wind actually would affect your hair and clothing. Consider the moments of your sudden dive—the CFX team actually pushed back your hair and rippled your clothing in the appropriate direction. Seconds later, when you pulled the machine out of its dive, they rearranged the dynamics on their computers and charted how you and Penny would look while ascending. Two different wind motions, two different effects.

SHERMAN: I'll never forget that dive! What does the other unit, the visual effects team, do?

MR. PEABODY: They create a realistic world in which the laws of motion and physics—of course, I aided them in this—apply to the scene with equal vigor. When you crashed Mr. da Vinci's plane into a tree, they directed each leaf to move according to the impact. The river you flew over naturally had to ripple and splash as it does in reality. This team creates the clouds and their movements, which I'm sure you and Penny hardly noticed, and manufactures effects such as fire, smoke, vapor, and the impressive light displays created by our travels in the WABAC. When character effects, visual effects, and the lighting team synchronize their efforts, the results are spectacular. In short, Sherman, if you can imagine it, they can do it.

SHERMAN: They certainly can, Mr. Peabody!

1, 4 • PEABODY PRODUCTION

2 • PEABODY FINAL LAYOUT & ANIMATION

3 • PEABODY LIGHTING

KEN PAK

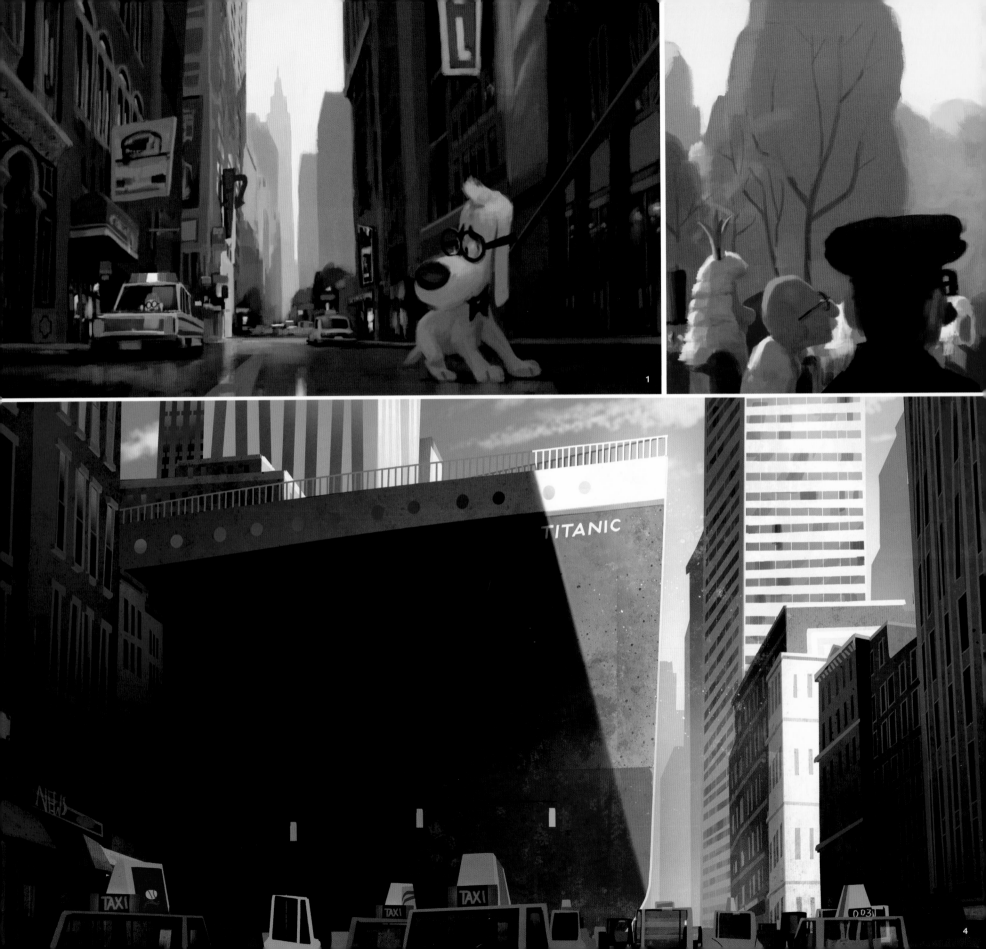

CONCLUSION

F rom humble beginnings in 1959, Mr. Peabody & Sherman have transcended their "guest star" roles in Rocky and Bullwinkle's cartoon show. They have also shed their two-dimensional existences and are now major 3D motion-picture stars in their own right. It couldn't have happened to a better dog—and his boy.

Director Rob Minkoff, producers Alex Schwartz and Denise Cascino, and DreamWorks' veteran production team kept Mr. Peabody & Sherman true to their irreverent origins while simultaneously stretching the boundaries of story and art, a delicate balancing act that only genuine fans of the original cartoons could accomplish. Had Jay Ward been able to see what heights his talking dog and adopted boy would reach in this film, he would have been amazed, amused, and very proud.

DreamWorks not only created an entertaining time-traveling adventure but touched the heart with a message for families of every description. To pull that together, the collaboration of the studio's own family of talents was key. All departments—from pre-vis to animation, editorial to lighting, character design to modeling—worked beautifully together to produce a final product that will live for a long time to come.

DreamWorks Animation has, in fact, much in common with their new stars, Mr. Peabody & Sherman. Creativity, imagination, vast technical knowledge, and a thirst for adventure are rich, shared traits. And both show no sign of slowing down: "Sherman, set the WABAC Machine for . . . the future!"

1–3 • CARLOS FELIPE LEÓN

4 • KEN PAK

5 • ZAC WOLLONS & BRYAN LASHELLE

6 • AVNER GELLER

7 • BRYAN LASHELLE

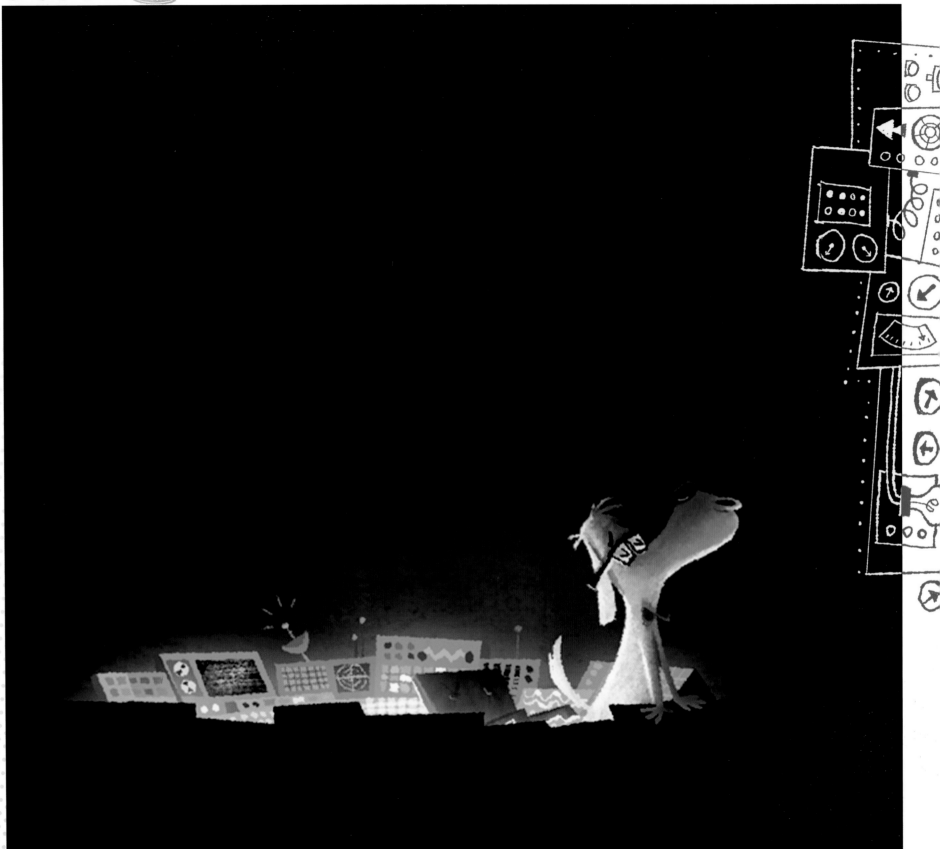

AFTERWORD

BY ROB MINKOFF

As you've seen, the making of *Mr. Peabody & Sherman* has been a labor of love for the hundreds of artists working at DreamWorks Animation. It took us nearly three years to complete the production, but the journey began many years before that.

Imagine if you will, stepping into the WABAC Machine and setting the dial for 2003. That's when executive producer Jason Clark walked into my office and asked, "Do you want to make a movie about Mr. Peabody & Sherman?" Without hesitation I said, "Yes!" The reason was, in the words of Mr. Peabody, "quite simple, really!" I wanted to do it because I loved the characters Jay Ward brought to life in his seminal television hit "Rocky and His Friends."

I remember watching their ironic, satirical adventures as a young child growing up in Palo Alto, California, never realizing the full impact they would eventually have on my own life. In fact, PDI-DreamWorks is only a ten-minute drive from the house I grew up in! And so I owe them a debt of gratitude. After all, Jay Ward and his family of zany characters partly inspired my own ambition to become an animator and filmmaker.

And perhaps this book, with its behind-the-scenes look at the making of *Mr. Peabody & Sherman*, will inspire a new generation of dreamers to turn their own fantasies into reality in the magical world of animation.

Rob Minkoff

5

2

3

4

ACKNOWLEDGMENTS

Special thanks to Bill Damaschke and Kristy Cox at DreamWorks Animation, Tiffany Ward at Bullwinkle Studios, Peabody's voice Ty Burrell, director Rob Minkoff, producer Alex Schwartz, and production designer David James for their contributions and assistance in making this manuscript magnifique.

To the *Mr. Peabody & Sherman* artists and staff, my thanks to Carly Stuart, Aubrey Millen, Denise Cascino, Walt Dohrn, Tim Lamb, Kent Seki, Laura Grieve, Joe Moshier, David Lipton, Philippe Denis, and Jason Schleifer for taking the time to chat with me about the production.

Kudos to my editor Roxanna Aliaga and art director Christine Kwasnik at Insight Editions for pulling this book together with such care and understanding.

For special efforts on behalf of this project, I want to thank my assistant Martin Goodman, colleagues Darrell Van Citters and Keith Scott, transcribers Dale Hoffer and Laura Fogelman, and my lovely lady, Yvette Kaplan.

—JERRY BECK

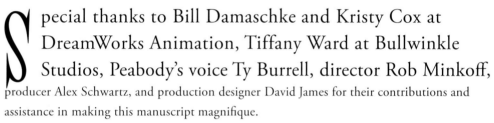

3

1 • GLENDALE CREW

2 • REDWOOD CITY CREW

3 • AVNER GELLER

COLOPHON

PUBLISHER Raoul Goff

ART DIRECTOR Chrissy Kwasnik

DESIGNER Jenelle Wagner

EXECUTIVE EDITOR Vanessa Lopez

EDITORS Roxy Aliaga and Elaine Ou

PRODUCTION MANAGER Jane Chinn

PRODUCTION EDITOR Rachel Anderson

INSIGHT EDITIONS would like to thank
Denise Cascino, Kristy Cox, Carlyn Siegler,
and Emma Whittard.

(PAGE 1) ALEX PUVILLAND & TIM LAMB; (PAGES 2–3)
SHANE PRIGMORE; (PAGES 6–7) KEN PAK, CARLOS FELIPE
LEÓN, AVNER GELLER & CHIN KO; (PAGES 26–27) KORY
HEINZEN; (PAGES 46–47) ALEX PUVILLAND; (PAGES
82–83) RUBEN PEREZ; (PAGES 122–123) TIM LAMB; (PAGES
136–137) KEN PAK

1–3 • PRISCILLA WONG

INSIGHT
EDITIONS

PO Box 3088
San Rafael, CA 94912
www.insighteditions.com

Library of Congress Cataloging-in-Publication Data available.

ISBN: 978-1-60887-258-9

Find us on Facebook: www.facebook.com/InsightEditions

Follow us on Twitter: @insighteditions

REPLANTED PAPER   ROOTS of PEACE

Insight Editions, in association with Roots of Peace, will plant two trees for each tree used in
the manufacturing of this book. Roots of Peace is an internationally renowned humanitarian
organization dedicated to eradicating land mines worldwide and converting war-torn lands into
productive farms and wildlife habitats. Roots of Peace will plant two million fruit and nut trees in
Afghanistan and provide farmers there with the skills and support necessary for sustainable land use.

Manufactured in China by Insight Editions

10 9 8 7 6 5 4 3 2 1